Am I a Racist?

Some Private Conversations Gone Viral

By Kurt Tyler

Copyright © 2018 by Kurt Tyler

All rights reserved worldwide.

No part of this publication may be replicated, redistributed, or given away in any form without the prior written consent of the author/publisher or the terms relayed to you herein.

Kurt Tyler, dcareerpaths@gmail.com or Twitter @kurtkattyler

ISBN 13: 978-0-9994043-4-8
ISBN 10: 0-9994043-4-2

Art design by Kurt Tyler

First Edition

Dedication

Thank-you God. The download was received.

Dedicated to my father Homer Duke Sr. and my mom Delma Louise, who as a team created the foundation for me to have a broad view of our world and a mindset in which I can now enjoy and be amazed living in a world of unique cultures.

About the Author

Kurt Tyler, is an Emerging Technologies, Innovation & Solutions Strategist with over thirty years of experience working with small through large businesses including corporations like General Electric (GE), Walgreens Booths Alliance and Freddie Mac.

Kurt's experiences include being a former producer of a nationally syndicated talk radio program hosted by Pulitzer Award recipient and renown author Studs Terkel, healthcare, finance and media industry assignments centered on merger and acquisition capability planning and integration, IT governance and compliance, client and vendor relationship management, e-commerce, virtual reality conceptualization, process improvement, behavior modification, mentoring, thought leadership, corporate strategy, collaborative team building, crisis management, conflict resolution, initiative management, music and broadcast production.

Author's Note

I hope this book can help at least one person with overcoming the fear of having meaningful, honest and engaging conversations about racism with their family, friends, acquaintances and most importantly, expanding those conversations beyond their private circles. In addition, I hope this book will give you at least one place to start. -KT

Table of Contents

Dedication 2

About the Author 3

Purpose 6

Chapter One: The Horror of Fear 11

Chapter Two: Conversations 24

    Hate, Fear, Discomfort, Normalcy 32

    I Don't Know (Why), I Just Do 43

    The Cold and Fatal Drink of Anxiety 48

Chapter Three: Implicit Bias, The Inception 53

    Two sources of Anxiety created by Bias 60

Chapter Four: You Can Run, but You Can't Hide, from History 64

    American Indian Nations 68

Chapter Five: Our Private Discussion 71

Chapter Six: Conclusion 77

    Shame, Guilt and Pain 78

    Closing Thoughts 87

Appendix: Considerations 91

Purpose

The purpose of this book is to share some private conversations that can be used as your personal self-assessment tool to gain better understanding of how you could be directly and indirectly involved with historic and systemic patterns and practices associated with racism.

One of the greatest challenges with gaining better awareness and detailed knowledge related to the circumstances associated with racism, is the fear and discomfort most people feel with being involved in a conversation between individuals belonging to different races, especially if there has been historic patterns and practices used by one against the other. Without some type of controlled platform and acceptable rules of engagement for discussion some might assume a discussion about racism will result in highly emotional verbal exchanges that will end up in a shutdown by one or both sides. The emotional exchanges can be caused by a perception that one or both sides are not listening to the other. There might also be a perception that one is not taking the discussion seriously or acknowledging their direct involvement with racist behaviors. Emotional stress can also be created by one or both sides not taking time to understand what are the psychological drivers behind their actions.

But there's at least one thing you can count on as an inseparable aspect aligned to racism. People seem to be the most comfortable having conversations about race and racism when they are having private conversations with their family, friends and close associates. That's when they really let loose. The privacy seems to allow people to feel comfortable sharing their innermost feelings especially when there is minimal expectation that the conversation will negatively impact their reputation or result in a heated discussion beyond what might be experienced when people talk about controversial topics.

Here's the revelation. Wouldn't it be beneficial if we were able to have open and honest conversations publicly? Conversations that are beyond the veil of privacy, similar to the ones many of us have with our families, friends and close acquaintances. Moving the conversations from behind closed doors and back rooms where true feelings are expressed, into the public space, needs to be our goal. This might take some time, but through print, we have the ability to share some conversations of what people are saying without exposing their names and addresses. This would be one approach for building towards having more open conversations between individuals, in the workplace and various public spaces.

This book is composed of outtakes from various private conversations I've heard over the years that included individuals belonging to different ages, cultures, nationalities and gender. I've included some of the questions that were raised during the conversations, responses, commentary, historic references, pertinent psychological research and a few of my own personal experiences. For the protection of their privacy and reputation, the identities of various individuals have been left anonymous. Fundamentally, this book was created to help you, the reader, increase your level of understanding and comfort with having public conversations focused on racism. In addition, it was created to share some perspectives that I hope will facilitate more discussion within your private conversations so that those conversations can move beyond the views often constrained by the limited number of participants, their knowledge and the level of exposure those participants have had with people outside their own race. In other words, having a conversation about the beliefs of a race of people when no one in the group has ever had a detailed conversation with an actual person belonging to that group will obviously be biased and lack credibility. Yes, it's true…there are still many people who have never spoken with someone of another race. In some geographically isolated countries it's possible they have never seen someone from another race. I've often wondered what would happen if someone stumbled into one of the secluded indigenous people of Brazil who are reportedly relying solely on nature for their social, health and nutritional vitality. There are also individuals who live in rural areas around the perimeter of vastly populated regions. Possibly their only exposure to other races, fiction or non-fiction, is from what they have seen on television. So, for those who rely on television for their education, you'll have to accept there is a large amount of information that station owners, network decision makers and advertising sales executives determine what is best for the public, after their product has been edited to their satisfaction. Unfortunately, the product that meets their satisfaction can also support their biases.

Knowing the potential constraints around your ability to receive balanced information from the media and if you've never experienced having engaging conversations about the values and beliefs of individuals who are not members of your race, how could you move beyond intrinsic bias and generalizations or be able to rely on the overall validity of what is discussed in closed conversations? How would you begin to realize what might be the actual cause of your concerns, fears, anger or anxieties? Has anyone brought this up during one of your private conversations?

Up to this point it has been customary and convenient to blame someone of another race as the sole reason why the accuser's personal goals or expectations can't be achieved. No one told them most people face similar challenges in life that they too will need to find solutions. If only they would have engaged in a simple conversation between others outside of their own race, they might have discovered the similarities being faced by both groups. No one informed them they have been living inside a social bubble where there are certain behaviors that have become normalized within the bubble, but still hurtful to others outside of the bubble. Possibly there are expected privileges inside the bubble that are not supported outside of it. What would you expect will happen as individuals venture out from their cocoons but have not been provided socialization skills or multi-cultural awareness. At some point awareness will be needed or conflict may occur. A perfect breeding ground for racism.

Many have already discovered when there is a lack of direct interactions between one or more races, it becomes easy to adopt beliefs, stereotypes or generalizations that are not true and possibly disrespectful. Once disrespect enters the mindset you can expect disrespectful actions until there is a re-education for those who have adopted false beliefs. Information and direct interactions are essential elements that allow others to gain the first-hand proof required to eliminate false beliefs and generalizations. Without open and honest conversations between individuals belonging to different races it becomes difficult to gain first-hand testimony to learn what are the actual beliefs that influence the behaviors of others. In addition, honest conversations can help clarify some of the motivating factors aligned to racist patterns and practices.

Another mindset that can contribute to incorrect beliefs and generalizations is when one race of people attempts to make an apples-to-apples comparison of their race to another even though there are clear social-economic differences that if all things were equal you might see both groups engaging in similar behaviors. In reality, all things are not equal. There are social-economic differences, bias and privileges that can impact the speed of one's ability to achieve their goals and expectations.

For instance, if one group is typically not hired into higher paid jobs resulting in the parents having to hold multiple jobs to make ends meet, that scenario may result in less one-on-one time available for raising their children. A group where one parent in the family leaves each day to go to work while the other works from home would present the opportunity for parents to spend more time raising their children and reinforcing healthy values. Social-economic factors could also be a motivating factor for why one group might consider riskier ways to gain income.

This book also has a goal of providing you the opportunity to have a private conversation with yourself. In doing so, it might be a surprise to discover those typically labelled as racist may not be the ones you would expect.

Also, since we currently live in a time where social media has the ability to effectively shine a spotlight on an increasing number of events that you find emotionally troubling, you may want to reach out to close friends or associates to have a private conversation that can allow the opportunity to express your anger, anxieties and frustrations. More importantly, I hope this book can assist in providing some therapeutic relief focused on healing. Here is a starting point for conversations and a path for moving forward towards a cure.

Chapter One: The Horror of Fear

Most people realize you can't have an honest conversation about racism without discussing the various fears of each individual.

There has not been one conversation on the subject of racism that didn't include statements concerning one or more fears concerning what their future might be if current practices changed. Depending on the impact of racism on you, there will either be statements to defend why things must remain the same or statements why things must change. Each statement is primarily motivated by fear. In some cases, individual fears are so emotionally intense that some individuals are horrified by the thought of living in a world where power is not in the hands of one race of people.

The internal struggle centers on the anxiety associated with concerns for what could happen if one's fears actually materialized. However, many initiate multiple courses of action focused on diminishing their fears by developing risk mitigation plans, also known as insurance plans. It's not unusual for people to build some type of insurance strategy to provide realistic options they believe can minimize various negative impacts if their fears began to materialize.

Since fear is a natural emotion evoked by the perception of danger, there is a tremendous body of guidance available to help lower the emotional anxiety associated with fear.

Yea though I walk through the valley of the shadow of death, I will fear no evil, for thou art with me... – The Holy Bible, Psalms 23:4

I learned that courage was not the absence of fear, but the triumph over it. The brave man is not he who does not feel afraid, but he who conquers that fear. – Nelson Mandela

We must constantly build dikes of courage to hold back the flood of fear. – Martin Luther King Jr's sermon, "Antidotes for Fear" in "Strength to Love"

Power does not corrupt. Fear corrupts... perhaps the fear of a loss of power. – John Steinbeck

You gain strength, courage, and confidence by every experience in which you really stop to look fear in the face. – Eleanor Roosevelt, You Learn by Living: Eleven Keys for a More Fulfilling Life

Courage is resistance to fear, mastery of fear, not absence of fear. – Mark Twain

If you know the enemy and know yourself you need not fear the results of a hundred battles. – Sun Tzu (6th century Chinese military strategist, author of the Art of War)

Fear defeats more people than any other one thing in the world. – Ralph Waldo Emerson

This world of ours, ever growing smaller, must avoid becoming a community of dreadful fear and hate, and be, instead, a proud confederation of mutual trust and respect. – Dwight Eisenhower, 1961 Presidential farewell to the nation address

Never say never, because limits, like fear, are often just an illusion. – Michael Jordan, 2009 Hall of Fame induction speech

Courage is knowing what not to fear. – Plato

Nothing in life is to be feared, it is only to be understood. Now is the time to understand more, so that we may fear less. – Marie Curie

During conversations on racism you will hear participants express some of the same fears that have been documented over and over throughout various points in history. There's the fear of payback. That translates into if power is transitioned into the hands of a race that has been dehumanized and treated unfairly, they will return the same to those who previously dealt out the racist practices. There's the fear of an even playing field. That translates into believing the group that previously enjoyed having advantages will no longer be able to enjoy being the most favored for receiving all benefits. They may possibly believe in the absence of favor they will become lowered to the level of being a commoner, having to compete for benefits the same as everyone else.

One of the questions I like to ask participants in conversations about racism is "what do you think the world would be like if people were treated fairly, and there was a level playing field instead of one group constantly getting favors." I like to follow-up with asking "can anyone cite a scenario where favoritism is not allowed, and what did that feel like?" Next, I like to ask "what about favoritism impacts you the most?" This question often results in silence, as individuals ponder back into their past. Searching for those moments in time when they received special treatment, received benefits and they were made to feel special, privileged or more important than others. How can you forget those enjoyable feelings? And you want more. The other perspective might be to consider all the circumstances where you knew you were just as special as someone else, but never received the opportunity to enjoy the benefits that were available. You didn't get special treatment or were told to wait. At this point you may begin to have more understanding, empathy of why some might experience a tremendous amount of fear and anxiety when considering having to manage so many aspects of life without someone giving them favors. This is a character of our lives and why there will always be those who seek to obtain new and maintain their existing favors, along with those who seek to obtain favor for the first time. There's apparently a basic innate desire to receive concierge service. Could this have developed from the days when you were a baby, relying on others to provide all of your needs? And that developed into wanting to be first in line, the first one chosen, to be treated better than others, to possess an abundance, to be the first to have access, to get the best deal, to enjoy exclusivity, to be the first to eat, to have the best care, to have the best job title, to have the highest salary, to have the best seats, to be the first to receive customer service, to be acknowledged beyond others. I could go on but I think you get the point.

Let's continue our conversation on racism, but now I'd like to add a new question. How do each of us, as individuals view privilege? This is where we begin to see the level of personal conviction exposed. How valuable is it to you to receive favor if favor results in partiality, and the partiality you receive is from someone with power? How important is it to you to have privilege if privilege will result in immunity from criminal charges, give you additional rights or benefits that others don't have? How far are you willing to go to maintain favor or privilege? What would you do to protect what you currently possess, or to obtain what you believe you deserve and are part of your rights? If you ask someone these questions, you will hear some key motivating factors that governs direct or indirect participation in racist patterns, practices and the measure of civility utilized.

Historically, the policies aligned to colonization and nation building included an 'anything goes' mentality when it came to usurping the benefits of land and its resources from the early inhabitants. We've seen military actions, embargoes, genocide, gentrification and various types of dehumanization to make acquisitionists feel it's alright to clandestinely or forcibly acquire resources and wealth previously owned by others. At this point should we ask how many believe racism is just a mask, a façade used to acquire and maintain wealth and power? How would you be impacted if the balance of wealth changed? How would you be impacted if those who are currently in power lost their influence? Well, due to the nature of human beings we can conclude favoritism will always exist. Privilege will change as more people gain wealth. Since wealth can be obtained through an unlimited number of paths, there is no way to really control or stop others from gaining wealth. In addition, we begin to see more individuals who don't rely on a race of people who may currently hold power, but instead on innovation, family businesses, valuable possessions rolled over through inheritance from one to whomever they favor. As others gain wealth, they also will determine who is on the guest list for a new emerging privileged class.

Given the fact that it is impossible to stop the acquisition of wealth, power, privilege and favoritism or for one group to block the transition of the same, one would also have to conclude the control of jobs and benefits will also change.

Now our conversation on racism shifts to address a different complexity. Some want to understand the reason why one race blames the other for allegedly plotting to steal the keys that unlock the door that controls permissions for individuals to enjoy benefits, receive favors and increase their prosperity. They blame others for their attempts to steal the keys, as if no one else should have the right to possess them. No one should proceed without receiving permission from the race that supposedly possess the keys. Is it possible that the mystery of who actually wields power at any given time, leaves many without clear answers and so they just blame the ones they hate? Shan't we blame the new kid on the block, the immigrants? Yes, let us blame them. And shan't we blame the bad kids on the block, the minorities? Yes, let us blame them, also. Are there any others we should blame? There must be. There's got to be someone to blame for the perceived fear of a pending loss of privilege, traditions, jobs and safety. Fear of losing control by the race who believe they hold the keys to power and prosperity.

Micro-managers may express discomfort or anger as their anxiety increases when they feel they are losing the ability to control everything. I recall one micro-manager ask me if I felt like things were getting out of control as the project we were governing began to expand to the point that it required additional resources to be hired. My response was "no," since I understood the project had expanded enough where we needed to delegate our authority over to others. We were no longer able to have direct hands-on management over every aspect of the project. We now needed others to be involved while we moved to a different level of oversight. The micro-manager continued to try to manage each aspect, be in every meeting, be on every call, and give out direction down to the fundamental level of each task. This micro-manager could not recognize their need to have control over others and quickly experienced increasing levels of anxiety. The manager soon learned the goal of having control over everyone was just impossible. This manager also began to experience failures due to a lack of acceptance. At some point micro-managers, like those who practice racism, will need to address their psychological need to have control over others. Especially when they really can't stop others from striving to build their own centers of controls.

Covert racism soon becomes more overt as racists begin to experience increasing levels of fears and anxieties. It seems to get worse as other races cut their dependencies while continuing to gain and hand over benefits to those they choose. Again, this is inevitable and not something one race has control over at all. They just believe they do. And yes, based on the level of conviction to retain power and traditions, we should expect to see an increasing number of overt actions that are manifestations of their anxieties. The behavior has the potential of continuing an upward trend in the absence of interdiction and treatment.

Historically, producers of racist actions were kept anonymous, but with the open shifts and perceived loss of controls we now witness their emotional pain played out in broad daylight. The pain from realizing changes taking place throughout the world that they can't stop. This is clearly a psychological issue that needs to be managed with professional guidance. The average person may not really know why they are feeling so much anxiety and hate towards another race. As more change materializes the stress level of the undiagnosed will probably continue. Hopefully it doesn't become an epidemic. But maybe it already has become an epidemic where you live.

During conversations I have to ask, "what is stopping individuals from continuing to practice their traditions with the exception of those that focus on dehumanizing others?" "What is stopping individuals from building wealth without relying on practices of oppression, being uncivil or being unfair to others?" "If other races can develop strategies to circumvent racist control-focused practices in-order to achieve their goals and expectations, why can't those who currently rely on racism, begin to develop strategies that are not dependent on racism in-order to ensure they can achieve their goals and expectations?" "Is there anything that is stopping businesses from exclusive hiring of whomever they choose, whether they prefer a staff that is comprised of a majority of men or women or from one race?" "Is there anything stopping business owners from only allowing men of one race to hold the top positions in a company?" "Is there anything stopping you from starting your own home business, building it over years, achieving your goals, expectations and creating jobs for your group?" "Is there anything that is stopping you from raising your family in the traditions you choose?" So, can we talk more about why some people believe the obstacles they face in life are caused solely by individuals from another race and not the various social-economic challenges that individuals within each community are working to overcome?

To put a different lens on the challenge people face with handling anxiety, many countries are experiencing some radical changes in trying to address national healthcare strategies. Health providers have realized there are high numbers living within their population that don't realize they are suffering from ailments and disease conditions that could be prevented or managed if only they were aware of preventative knowledge. As a result, health providers have initiated various solutions to help educate the public about simple everyday practices that could prevent the onset of health issues. In the absence of basic information, individuals have been experiencing adverse outcomes including death.

If only they were aware of simple practices, they potentially could increase their odds of having long and healthy lives. The key is they need to have access to health providers who can educate, advise, prevent and manage issues early. But since healthcare providers have realized access is an obstacle for many, they have implemented public education through media channels and free public events. Some are going out from their physician offices and into communities and regions to extend care and education. For the national healthcare debate, the anxiety is around the need to change existing payment practices and the need to re-educate populations. Health providers moving out from their offices and into the field is critical for lowering anxieties.

This is a similar scenario for those who blame others for their fears of something not actually materialized. They are experiencing so much rapid change in power, wealth, benefits, privilege and who controls jobs over what seems like a short period of time, when in fact it has been happening over decades. The diagnosis and management of increasing levels of anxiety and anger has yet to effectively reach the public. Part of the management includes filling a tremendous void with awareness.

Through our conversations on racism you may be able to gather clues as to why you are feeling so much anger, hatred and lack of civility towards a specific race, group or individual. Through conversations it begins to become apparent these feelings are not exclusive to one race. But the next step is to begin to address how to adjust, become tolerant of other's desire to grow, and if necessary, obtain personal guidance. Relying on the strategy of oppressing others is proving not to be a viable long-term strategy since those being oppressed will, and are finding solutions to circumvent racist patterns and practices.

I would hope the public awareness approach that healthcare providers are doing to educate their populations on preventative health practices, could be duplicated by psychiatrists who can initiate strategies to educate populations on managing the need for controlling others, managing the associated fears, anxiety and mis-directed anger towards others. A generalized population health strategy that provides guidance from psychiatrists can begin to help individuals gain better understanding into why they have a need to extend control over others beyond the control they have as individuals and families.

In conversations I would urge participants to discuss what exactly they believe will happen as other races build their own wealth, bases of power, disperse benefits, create jobs and increase the number of those with privilege. Do participants believe their benefits will actually disappear even though their race is continuing to build upon their current position? I would agree, as more people establish their own bases of power, the existing power structures will probably need to incorporate growing numbers whom they may need to negotiate. However, there will also be those areas where benefits continue to be controlled exclusively by an individual or group. That would mean there may not be a noticeable impact to you directly.

In reality, those who are experiencing increasing levels of anxiety as they witness more of racist strategies fail, are overlooking there is nothing stopping their ability to enjoy benefits, privilege and favor. They must strive at overcoming their personal fears. Afterall, they will still be able to go to their favorite store or restaurant and receive enjoyable customer service. They will continue to find businesses that prefer to hire only certain people. They will continue to have people pull them aside to tell them about a way to obtain a great deal or benefit that others may not have identified. They will continue to be invited to take part in exclusive events, memberships and opportunities. They will continue to have judicial and legislative decisions issued in their favor. They will continue to get into schools or get a job because someone gave them a recommendation.

To sum it up, privilege and favors will always exist and will not disappear. What we are now experiencing is the culmination of strategies implemented over decades where various race groups have learned to build their own bases of power, start their own businesses, create jobs, build wealth and begin to determine who they prefer to provide privileges and favors. Their actions are partly the equal and opposite action cited in Newton's third law. The shock for those who have been utilizing racism to hinder others is materializing in their sudden realization that individuals no longer need to rely on one race to obtain prosperity or give them benefits. They have created their own. Even for those having reached the realization, it still may not make sense to them how individuals who have been under the yoke of racism used to control and keep them in their place, now have luxury vehicles, now have powerful positions, now can afford to travel first-class, now can become the President of the United States. In many cases change emerged from the bottom up. Those families who had to endure unfair and dehumanizing behavior were some of the ones who quietly put long-term plans in place for their families. They put savings aside to ensure their children completed higher learning. Afterwards, those children re-invested in their families and in community development programs. For racist, they feel as though they have lost control. The lesson to be learned is you can't keep disrespecting people forever. At some point in time their quiet strategies will begin to emerge and show results. And they will continue to build, grow, invest, innovate, establish their own business clients, evolve and overcome abusive and oppressive behaviors because it is not how they want to live.

For some they may resolve their anxiety is driven by the belief they personally are responsible to keep certain groups of people 'in their place.' Or they incorrectly believe some groups are not smart enough to know how to become successful or have positive values. Or they fear their current traditions and way of life will be lost. Of course, these feelings would be based on applying their own individual criteria on others, which is a clear attempt to extend their control over others. But history is proving this strategy is not a viable one. Enlightenment for racist comes upon realizing that they cannot control everyone's fate, ability to thrive nor block one of the strongest desires in human beings. The desire to enjoy life and to do all they can to make life better for their children. You can't stop that.

In the past racism was used to ensure the retention of a way of life and traditions for one race of people. A way of life that oppressed people belonging to one or more races in-order to ensure that the abundance of benefits remain in the hands of one group. Is it possible there are some who fear at some point all available benefits will run out, innovation will stop and no new benefits, resources and wealth will ever be available? So, maybe I shouldn't ask what is the purpose of the increasing investments in space exploration, the ocean, green energy or technology research and development? Each of those investments would seem to support the probability of consistent increases of new discoveries and opportunities.

Conversations on racism must include discussions focused on the worldwide challenge to establish and retain a long-term income stream, a job or a career. Keep in mind this is not just a challenge in the area, neighborhood, town, city or country where you live, but a worldwide challenge. The majority of people around the world feel anxieties associated with the challenge of establishing and maintaining long-term income streams. When the money is coming in the anxiety often shifts to a fear of not having enough to pay bills or to put enough aside for the future. When the income stream is missing there is often the need to find someone to blame, not considering there are many factors including individual biases that determine who is hired. Those biases are within the minds of everyone, not just the race of people who is the racist's target of the week, month or year. There are many players in the game of acquisition, conquest, power and manipulation. People belonging to one race are not exclusive to needs, but are often the convenient, low risk group used as the focus of blame, for the hardships of others, even when they know nothing of your hardships, because they are focused on their own.

So, we've discussed how some people believe racism and anxiety work together. And the anxiety increases as those formerly oppressing others realize they can no longer retain control over those they formerly oppressed. There also is anxiety from a belief that those who were formerly oppressed will retaliate upon leveling the balance of power. The anxiety. The fears. The anger. All because of increasing evidence confirming the strategy to implement control over one or more races, is crumbling, is being circumvented, is being defeated, broken or lost. At some point those who don't look within their selves to address their own need to keep up with a changing world, will find they are sitting in their private bubble filled with anxiety, anger and fears while those who realize and embrace change will innovate, learn how to benefit from new opportunities as they continue to emerge.

Chapter Two: Conversations

I've been fortunate to have been in the midst of a number of private conversations between family members, close friends and acquaintances who were discussing various events characterized as being racist. I found these conversations extremely provocative and evidently others do too because I'm noticing talking points similar to what have been discussed in these private conversations are beginning to circulate in wider circles. Possibly this is the six degree of separation effect. It's also interesting that the individuals involved in these private conversations have been a mix between street smart, college educated, different ethnicities, age and genders, but all intelligent men and women who rely on a set of principles and experiences to guide their lives. I suspect this is the reason why the conversations are never the same and always leave participants with an increased awareness.

What a controversial topic, powerful question and label. A conversation many hope to avoid, but in the back of your mind you know at some point it will probably happen and you may feel you are only prepared to discuss your own feelings and points of view. That realization often leaves individuals with an uncomfortable fear in their gut of not knowing what others actually feel and will say during a face-to-face conversation. The fear of the mere mention during a conversation could evoke strong emotions that might result in immediate retreats into invisible defensive shells or can immediately stimulate the recollections stored hidden in memories of events experienced at any point in time. The word racist and the knowledge of racism can motivate many to attempt living most of their life avoiding honest discussions with anyone with the exception of those who share their similar perspectives or upbringing. For others this word can be forever tethered to a memory of humiliation, embarrassment, shame, guilt, anger and discomfort. Unfortunately, even if you were the giver or receiver, you probably will prefer to avoid conducting a thorough self-analysis that could identify and address your own behavioral triggers that are impacting how you interact with others. That avoidance to look inwardly will probably continue unless you hear the four words many hope they would never hear. You are a racist!

Upon hearing those words, now the unofficial trial begins. The accuser presents their case by revealing evidence of something they heard or something they witnessed. The evidence may be a video or audio recording that seems to support their claim. Then the accused responds with a firm denial proclaiming, "I am not a racist!" I have friends who are of that race. That response, which is not much of a defense, is followed by laughter from the accuser. Who are those friends? Bring them forward so we can ask about your relationship with them and find out how you treat them. Now if your friends never show up, the trial is concluded and the accusation is confirmed, resulting in a scarlet letter 'R" of shame being attached to you forever. But in some cases, a few acquaintances step forward only to repeat your original statement that you are not a racist, and possibly citing the good things you have done for them. Unfortunately, your friends have overlooked this is a defense that has never been accepted as proof, so that too is challenged by the accuser with a demand to explain the recorded evidence that captured your racist behavior. Adding your actions are similar to previously documented racist practices conducted by others throughout history. The courtroom is silent, collectively holding their breath while waiting for the explanation. None is given. The trial is concluded with either the accused angrily walking away, having been 'outed' and shamed, or with the accused issuing a brief apology as a damage control tactic focused on minimizing their reputational risk where the fine could be exile, resulting in the need for everyone publicly associated with you to cut their ties or face the risk of being dragged down with you, by association. Branded! You are a racist!

But is it possible you just didn't know your actions were associated with historically racist patterns or practices? Could you have been taught early in life certain practices without awareness of the harmful history aligned to those same practices? Or in reality, do you just believe certain people should be treated harshly, and put in their place? Maybe you believe there's a certain order of things and you've been personally ordained to enforce them. These perspectives turn on a hot spotlight that's focused directly on the missing details and expands the depth of the conversation. A conversation that takes place privately or in an unofficial trial. Have you actually thought about the perspective you hold, and more importantly, why? What is really at the center of your view and what is driving it?

For many people it is easier and more comfortable to retreat behind claims that political correctness has gone too far. For others each occurrence highlights the continual need to learn of, and be knowledgeable of practices that are disrespectful and are used to dehumanize others so they don't repeat them. For most people it really doesn't take much thought to conclude that continual unresolved racism can result in stress, anger, conflict, discomfort, anxiety, violence, uncertainty and unexpected reactions. Instead of citing political correctness gone too far, you should ask, is a racist world really what you want to live in? A world where one group finds it acceptable to be mean-spirited, disrespectful, uncivil and dehumanizing to others.

So, the question is why does racism continue? Some might answer there are practices that were acceptable when they were growing up. But those who use that perspective as a defense would also have to ignore the probability that during the time when they were growing up, racism was so entrenched in their area that it was perceived to be a normal acceptable behavior by those who practiced racism. As a result of those on the receiving end having so few remedies to obtain fairness, they often just turned the cheek, had no other choice but to tolerate racism. They avoided confrontation and were forced to accept dehumanization. Historically there were and still continue to be practices and tools in place to reinforce a behavior of acceptance by those on the receiving end of racism. In the past the controlling groups also used tools designed to punish or make an example of those who uttered a single word of protest.

From the political arm Jim Crow laws were put in place to maintain racist practices. From the judicial arm the courts would and continue to ignore or excuse racist patterns and practices. In addition, judges have been known to hand out harsher punitive damages in their attempt to squash any public complaining about unfair treatment by the judge, lawyers and law enforcement employees. Additional behavior modification has been seen in the forms of physical destruction to personal property, loss of employment, reputational character assassinations, hangings, harassment, intimidation and overzealous use of police authority which often led to frivolous arrests and increased incarceration of individuals of a specific race. With all of those constrictive practices in place it shouldn't be much of a surprise why racism appeared to be a normal behavior that included a clear absence of protests and complaints. For those growing up in that period it's a possibility they were not made aware or had any understanding of the impacts of those practices. They may have thought hangings and extreme violence directed on a specific race was because those targeted had done something wrong or were people who deserved public humiliation and discipline. In addition, those implementing racist practices in those times probably never had any concerns that their practices were disrespectful and inflicted harm. Fast forward years later to today, for those individuals who were raised in a racist environment but have not increased their awareness and empathy over years, they may not understand why people might be upset. For those stuck in the past, it could have been their choice to live in the racist ways of the past, living within a bubble or on an isolated knowledge desert. However, now those targeted by racists have new defensive tools and are increasingly fighting back when confronted with racist practices from the past.

I also suspect racism continues because there are two conflicting book-end mindsets, with various degrees between them. One mindset belongs to people who find satisfaction with doing things that bring harm to others. The easiest targets of their scorn might be people who they believe don't share their same values or are members of a different tribe or culture. People having this antagonistic mindset might be identified by their anger, hatred for others, extreme fears, social isolation, insecurities, bullying, disrespect for others or their need to blame others for the obstacles they encounter throughout life.

The other group typically has a mindset where they don't find much need to dedicate time planning ways to harm people. If you belong to this latter group you have to guard yourself from being used as a tool by the antagonistic group to carry out plans designed to harm others. You might need to look inward to determine what have you done and are doing to isolate yourself from racist patterns and practices?

I often ask myself, why do some people feel that having more than one culture, race or ethnic group in this world is a bad thing? Or what makes people believe there should only be one race that has power over all the other races of the world?

For the few who are so bold as to dive into this controversial subject, they begin to develop into a unique group of people having a heightened sense of awareness concerning the people around them. They realize there are some very distinct categories or frames of mind when it comes to how individuals are involved with racism or are labeled as being racist.
1. There are those who are proud racists.
2. There are those who are covert racists in that they anonymously support the overt patterns and practices of racists while they simultaneously hope to maintain a socially responsible reputation or to appear as having separation from the patterns and practices which will enable their ability to claim plausible deniability.
3. There are those who participate in racist patterns and practices but don't realize it.
4. There are those having a heightened awareness who have a universal respect for the rights, values and practices of those belonging to different races, as long as they don't bring hurt to others.

As a member of one of many groups worldwide who can attest they have been recipients of racist behavior, I've confirmed during conversations with friends belonging to a different race and culture there are times when they were unaware that some of their actions could be considered to be racist and it was not their intent to be disrespectful or provide harm to people belonging to a different race and culture. I recall a co-worker of a different race once asked me to pronounce a certain word that some have been known pronounce by placing the accent in a different location than those in their race. Knowing this was a racial generalization, I pronounced the word placing the accent the same as their race tend to place it. The response, "you're not like the others." I laughed, all the time knowing she was frustrated not hearing what she had expected to hear. Something her friends had spoken about in their private conversations on race and now she was trying to obtain proof. I knew she really didn't know she was making a racist generalization in believing everyone in my race spoke the same. She and those in her private conversation didn't consider there are dialects or there are individuals whose families originated from different regions of the country and world, each of which holding on to the pronunciations taught in their region and the way of communicating that distinguishes who they are. I realized there are some who believe the only correct pronunciations are those their group uses. I also knew there are broad differences in pronunciations between American English, British English as well as how English is spoken around the world. Those differences include where accents are applied. And so, I laughed.

Here's another one. I viewed a post on social media that brought attention to how it's possible to have done something that is considered racist by the recipient, while the individual who initiated the action was actually unaware of the results of their actions. This included wearing clothes, adopting hairstyles or using slang in a way that imitates characteristics associated with another race. Possibly playing a specific genre of music believed to gain acceptance. These are all friendly gestures but can also be recognized as generalizations believed used by all members of a race. And when I canvassed a number of my friends and family members regarding this specific scenario, I found a variety of responses that seemed driven based on their age, race, personal level of tolerance and acceptance, their experiences with racist circumstances, level exposure to diverse cultures, knowledge of world history, traditional family values & practices, parental 'talks' or problem-solving guidance provided by someone hoping to protect their loved ones. As a result, I began to wonder could it be that over time racism has become such a normal element within some of our lives that we've become desensitized to some events and therefore ignore them while only responding to the more egregious and extreme interactions. Could certain ethnic slurs or offensive statements be increasingly ignored and just considered to be the language used by someone deemed unenlightened or ignorant? Could excessive policing practices and patterns targeting a racial group be deemed by civic and judicial leaders acceptable based on current levels of tolerance. Has the acceptance of overt hiring discrimination reached a point that there is no longer any hope of obtaining legal remedies when businesses openly refuse to hire fairly or provide services to specific racial groups?

The more I thought about potential changes to the acceptable levels of tolerance, I began to tackle how I might be able to provide more clarity around this often-heated subject. While going down the path to identify how someone might be labeled as racist, I made an unexpected discovery. When I began thinking about my co-worker's racist generalization where she expected me to pronounce a specific word as she expected everyone in my race would pronounce the word, I began to realize in some cases, I too could be labeled as a racist. I too have made statements in ignorance of how my statements could be hurtful to a specific ethnic or racial group. In those cases, I can admit there was no intent to harm, but was unaware of the hurt that could have been transmitted. Upon gaining awareness I made a commitment not to repeat the statements that I became aware could be classified as being racist.

With this understanding I realized there probably are people who might be labeled as a racist but honestly don't welcome being associated with that group and are challenged with the question of how to improve their personal image. For those who might seek but are struggling with finding solutions they can utilize, I thought it might be helpful to sharing some details from conversations focused on assisting, at least one person who is interested in gaining more understanding on the subject that can be a private thought-provoking, put your toe in the water type of tool that can present that one person, options in a fashion where they can gain perspectives without having to deal with confrontational face-to-face discussions that could potentially escalate to an uncomfortable level. I suspect there are many who would welcome calm and relaxed discussions that could allow them to learn the intricacies of different races and could facilitate a world having fewer personal conflicts. I also suspect few would sign up for being in a discussion where yelling at each other is part of the process.

The Merriam-Webster Dictionary defines racism to be:
1. A belief that race is the primary determinant of human traits and capacities and that racial differences produce an inherent superiority of a particular race.
2. A doctrine or political program based on the assumption of racism and designed to execute its principles.
3. A political or social system founded on racism.

In each of these definitions, race is the foundational factor used in implementing specific actions.

Hate, Fear, Discomfort, Normalcy

Throughout the course of being a participant in conversations regarding racism I began to recognize there were four categories that I was able to place each conversation. Potentially there might be more but here are the ones I consistently heard. Hate, fear, discomfort and normalcy. Within each of these drivers many people, globally, might find they are aligned. As a result, individuals could potentially participate in racist behaviors in various degrees, falling anywhere between extreme through minimal behaviors.

There are those whose behaviors are solely driven by **hate**. For those individuals there are potentially an unlimited number of reasons why they hate someone of a different race. Their hate could be the result of an actual experience, something taught, learned biases, fear of losing control over others, concerns that others are no longer acknowledging their long-standing or historical traditions, fear that others are impacting the number of available jobs, concern they will no longer command preferential treatment, uncomfortable with increasing numbers of people belonging to other races changing the racial dynamics or fear another race is hindering their ability to receive benefits. It appears those whose behaviors are driven by hate are the ones who can be driven by all four drivers. Hate, fear, discomfort and normalcy.

There are those behaviors that are driven by **fear**. In those cases, individuals may not have hate, but are afraid of individuals belonging to a specific race. Their fear could be the result of a lack of information, having a lack of exposure or limited opportunities to get to know individuals from other races or having acceptance in characterizations, propaganda or having knowledge of a high visibility event that was attributed to one or more individuals who are members of a specific race. They might also be concerned for potential repercussions, guilt or shame knowing someone in their immediate family or ancestors hurt others. This group might be more influenced by stereotypes or biased generalizations until they experience having direct interactions that allow them to shed false beliefs.

There are those whose behaviors are the result of having a feeling of **discomfort** being around individuals belonging to a specific race. For some reason they feel uncomfortable with individuals of a specific race being within their safe zone. That intrusion could be perceived as a breach of their personal space or within a perceived border zone surrounding their geographic region. Discomfort could also be the result of believing in generalizations, stereotypes, implicit bias or that one race of people is the cause for an interruption of a comfortable pattern. For example, I've heard statements like "those people always drive slowly." In reality, the discomfort is the result of a perceived interruption for those who like to drive fast. The statement that is actually a generalization and could be classified as being a racist statement, was probably not motivated by hate or made with an intent to hurt or bring harm to the race of focus, but more of a racist statement motivated by personal inconvenience. Another example I've heard focuses on people voicing their discomfort with being around men of a particular race whenever they drink too much beer. Statements consistently note how there is an expectation they will become belligerent, unruly, rude, and could start fights when they drink excessively. Individuals belonging to various races voice warning to their friends to be cautious when men of this specific race are at American football or Association football matches known as soccer, popular bar areas on Saturday nights, some traditional annual celebrations and ethnic focused parades. These statements are clear generalizations that could be deemed as being racist statements driven by discomfort believed to be created by men of a specific race. However, hate doesn't seem to be the central motivating driver for these statements. Discomfort and possibly the fear of getting involved in a brawl seem to be the dominant drivers.

Lastly, there are those who behaviors are driven as a result of a level of **normalcy** being established where historically racist behaviors are considered to be normal behaviors. In these cases, individuals may not be motivated by hate, have any need to hurt, bring harm or instill control over people of one race or another. Their involvement, directly or indirectly is more the result of the environment where they were raised or currently reside. They might be considered to be naïve to knowing that they are doing something that has been historically associated as being a racist behavior. Within those bubbles, individuals have adopted and accepted some behaviors that they believe are normal ways in which they can interact with people of a specific race. For example, in some regions of the United States of America some white Americans don't find it disrespectful to address a grown African-American man as "boy" because they have addressed them in that manner for hundreds of years. It's become a norm for many due to decades of reinforced behavior. Another example might be how some individuals treat low paid domestic or farm workers without extending much respect or dignity. Some might be treated as though they are uneducated. But why should their work or income be an excuse to disrespect people? I've personally have witnessed some adult domestic workers being spoken to as though they were children.

Another area where normalization of racist depictions is widespread is in the practice of wearing costumes or having sports mascots that characterize other races for fun, ignoring their characterizations are hurtful and dehumanizing to a specific race. During sports events there can be depictions of sacred tribal ceremonies of indigenous people like American Indians or others, trivialized. I've often wondered if there is actually an American Indian tribe called 'The Redskins' or 'The Reds'. I don't believe so. The normalcy here is there are sports teams having those exact names that are offensive terms and by definition 'Redskin' is a racial slur. Would it be appropriate to have a sports team named using offensive terms like 'The Indianapolis Whiteshins' or 'The San Francisco Yellows or Japs' or 'The Chicago Coons' or 'The Boston Bog-Jumpers'? How about 'The Manhattan Dagos' or 'The Miami Caucazoid Crackers'? I think there would be a quiet of an uproar if any of those names were applied to a sports team. But Redskins, that's ok. We've seen white individuals put on black-face make-up, which was originally made popular in the early 1800's by an actor who as part of his entertainment show, created a character that reportedly depicted a physically handicapped black man (crooked leg and deformed shoulder), appearing as uneducated and stupid wearing torn clothes, while dancing and singing to the audience. His black-faced character was dehumanizing but white audiences found his act extremely enjoyable to watch and so the black-faced characterizations of black people spread widely as entertainment for one race only. Approximately 100-years later individuals continue to find it acceptable to dress up while wearing black-face make-up, revising this dehumanizing character. I think if some people realized the black-faced entertainers were poking fun at a man who was reportedly physically handicapped, they might think differently about dressing up in black-face make-up. Some individuals are too young to know the history and others may remember when they were children, some black-faced performers based on the 1928 Amos and Andy radio program and jazz singer, Al Jolson singing "Mammy" were recognized as famous entertainers. As such, they probably see the characterization as legendary entertainment for white Americans, but don't see it represents dehumanization to African-Americans. For Halloween we often see individuals wearing costumes that unfavorably depict various races.

If you might be wondering if you could be characterized as being a racist, here are a few questions. Have you ever made a decision that would result in one or more racial groups having difficulty receiving benefits of some type (E.g.: Employment; critical information; insurance; approval of a loan; communicating the availability of benefits; recognition; promotions; quality education; fair arbitration to resolve a disagreement; fair restitution after an unfair act or a loss.)? When deciding who you will vote for do you typically support the candidate that you expect will ensure your race or ethnic group receives the abundance of public benefits over other groups (E.g.: Schools; infrastructure; health systems; safety; improvements)? Do you believe one racial group requires more discipline than others or that same group is typically involved with criminal activities? As a result, do you believe they need to be kept separated from you (by community, railroad tracks, gated communities) and heavily policed?

Premise One. Once an individual is publicly labeled as a racist, their initial response is denial, possibly due to their concern for how the label could impact their economic, political or social image. As additional support of this premise I find it interesting that I've never heard of anyone who has been labeled a racist, then owning it and openly declaring, "yes, I am a racist." I've never heard one. Instead, the common response has been defensive responses, indifference, deflective actions, confrontation, anger or just totally ignoring the accusations.

Premise Two. There is a common practice that many of us are guilty. It is the practice of relying predominantly on our assumptions. During conversations with people that you don't know, we rely on our own customs during these encounters without considering there is a high probability that you may say something or do something that is offensive to others as a result of not knowing their cultural beliefs and practices. Many of us overlook that it is impossible to know what are the customs and beliefs held dearly by individuals raised in different cultures. And without this awareness we assume there is some type of universal cultural norms. For example, we might assume when you meet someone it is alright to shake hands. But there are some cultures where a bow from the waist is customary instead of a handshake. And if you are not mindful, you could easily offend someone from a different culture as a result of not asking about what are appropriate practices for interacting with people of different cultures. Being enlightened with this understanding, I find in my initial interactions with people of different cultures I prefer to communicate a subtle disclaimer explaining my concern that since I don't know the customs held dearly by someone, I could unknowingly offend them. I've found after communicating this disclaimer the individual acknowledges that truth of the mutual risk and that simple exchange initiates a sharing of key information focused on providing a safe path.

As support to this premise here are a few customs I've become aware that are held dearly by different cultures. While in the presence of elders you should remain silent until invited to speak. For some you should never hug someone from the opposite sex when greeting them. For some cheek kisses one on their right then one on their left cheek is accepted. Never kiss on the first date. Don't bring politics into initial discussions. In some cultures, you should expect to be asked very personal questions while others you should avoid asking personal questions until you have established trust. Some cultures you should not take credit for your achievements but instead honor those who facilitated your achievements. In some cultures, the dinner host should serve their guests first before eating where other cultures first set all the food on a table and after blessings everyone goes for the food like being in a battle or follow buffet style line ups, one behind the other.

As you might imagine, without having some knowledge and respect for understanding what is or not appropriate could easily result with being branded with a negative label up to and including being racist. If you are not aware or have any concern for what is offensive to another race you could be labeled a racist by those who are aware of the breach. The simple cure for this scenario would be to apologize for the indiscretion and then avoid recurrences. The key being, if you were knowledgeable you should have some sense of humanity not to knowingly do something that brings harm or pain to another human being.

Premise Three. Only those who are knowledgeable of the cultural practices of a race of people or aspects that the same group finds offensive have the foundational capability to determine if someone is involved with racist practices or activities. And in concluding the racist label is appropriate there should have been an evaluation by the individual or group that was offended or harmed that was based on witnessing consistent practices and policies when it has been determined the offender knows what are disrespectful to a culture. If the individual or group offended expresses harm, how can anyone not in that group claim that group has not been harmed? This is distinctly different when someone has unknowingly offended someone who is a member of a specific race.

Premise Four. This is a bit more obvious. When someone knows that certain words, phrases, symbolism, policies and practices will be disrespectful or probably result in hurt or damage to a specific race of people or culture, that person fits the definition of a racist. And if that person has no regrets and is comfortable being involved with practices focused on implementing harm to people belonging to a specific race or culture you could also be considered an invisible or covert conspirator or facilitator engaged in racist policies and practices. And although you may have personal reasons why you are engaged with those activities, the mere fact that you gain emotional fulfillment in a practice of harming people highlights a deeply personal and psychological problem.

Premise Five. There can be a number of reasons why individuals make racist statements. As a result of those statements, those same individuals could be branded as being a racist.

For example, expressing your dislike for a practice that is different from your individual practice or one associated with your own racial group when your statement targets one racial group, could be considered as racist. In this case your statement may not be based on hate but more on your level of tolerance for others to be different. For example, you might speak in private or public about how people of a certain racial group are always loud in public, disrespectful to others by playing their music loud or talk in a theater while others are trying to watch a movie. But for anyone who has lived in a campus dormitory, an apartment building or densely populated community you are aware that high noise levels, loud talking, parents shouting at their children and people shouting to get the attention of someone are all practices utilized by people of from a variety of racial groups. Stating that people from one racial group always drive their automobiles slow could also be considered to be a racist statement that is not driven by hate against the entire group but a discomfort received that is blamed on one group. In some areas this discomfort has resulted in laws passed to discourage slower drivers from driving in the lanes utilized by fast drivers. In addition, express lanes have been designated to accommodate drivers who tend to drive fast.

Another example would be where your statement is driven by hate. In this case a statement might be the result of hearing other statements conveyed having the goal to teach and recruit others through publicly orchestrated or private messaging from individuals. If the individual has had zero or limited opportunities to confirm the validity of the messaging against the targeted racial group it becomes easy to build their hate when separatist practices relies on ensuring there are missing blocks of interactions and actual experiences that would empower individuals with the ability to discern when they are receiving hate focused messaging.

Another example would be where your statement is the result of a negative experience you had with someone of a different racial group. And as a result, that one experience has manifested into a generalization against each and every individual associated with that group. For example, if each time you are interviewed for a job and not hired it's easy to make racist statements towards all interviewers who are from one racial group even though it could be the company not the interviewer that supports a long-standing practice of hiring only individuals from one racial group. Another example might be if someone from a racial group gave you poor customer service. You might make racist statements about the same group even though the practice for how a customer is treated is driven from the top leadership down to those who have direct contact with customers.

Premise Six. Utilization of others to conceal their identity from the public and if discovered can provide a plausible deniability alibi for those who systemically practice racism. Some common practices can materialize through the utilization of law enforcement, creation of biased laws and appointment of like-minded judges all to provide a veil for racist to hide behind while carrying out their racist behaviors. So, voting for or supporting people known to have bias against specific racial groups, even though you are hidden behind a veil of anonymity, would make you a racist. The veil of anonymity only allows you the ability to deny you are a racist and can allow you to cite that you have acquaintances who are members of the targeted racial group. The veil of anonymity can potentially make it difficult for accusers to present proof of your racist behaviors but there is always someone that can testify of one's actions or point of views, historic patterns, practices and individual character.

For example, back-door accusations and character assassinations are often used to create obstacles for individuals belonging to a targeted racial group. Another example might be to place anonymous calls to police as a tactic to use police officers as their personal tool for delivering their bias or hate. By hiding behind the veil of anonymity the obvious hope is to be able to repeatedly attack someone without the person knowing where the attack originated.

So, in each of the premises cited you could be labeled as being racist as result of a statement, practice, lack of tolerance, level of discomfort or attempt to remain anonymous. In each case you may not consider yourself as being racist but it's the recipient of your actions who will apply the label without having insight into what was the circumstance that motivated your statement or actions.

Unfortunately, many are still struggling with having truthful conversations, publicly or individually, about their motivation, but instead retreat into denials, defensive responses, indifference, deflective actions, confrontation, anger or just totally ignoring the accusations.

Do you think you, your friends, or associates may have a point of view that could possibly be an honest attempt to reconcile implicit bias or increase racism I.Q., but may find it awkward without actually having a mechanism to discuss, share, learn, gain feedback and awareness of successful methods to navigate?

I Don't Know (Why), I Just Do

There are also numerous race-related abuses of authority that individuals are confronted with on a daily basis while at their workplace. I recall an experience where I was the target of a racially-biased manager who each time she saw me she would assign me custodial cleaning duty in an attempt to dehumanize me, since she knew I was a manager responsible for assignments to support the senior manager who incidentally was also the manager of the racially-biased manager. Since her actions put me in direct conflict with my assigned responsibilities from the senior manager who had the higher authority, I spoke with the senior manager to inform her that each day after she gave me my assignments, the other manager would show up and countermand her directives, citing her assignments were what was needed at the moment even though we had staff who were specifically hired to handle custodial cleaning duty. Upon hearing her directives were being countermanded the senior manager called a meeting with the three of us to reinforce her line of authority. During this meeting the senior manager explained the importance of the assignments she was giving to me but also sensed there was something a bit odd about her daily re-assignment for me to handle custodial cleaning duties when we had staff for those exact responsibilities. She began to cautiously probe into the reasons behind her decision. In addition, the senior manager discussed the need for managers to work together and if a situation develops requiring reassignments, they need to be approved by her, the senior manager. And then came the defining period in which the senior manager paused to hear the racially-biased manager respond. I could see the junior manager tense up while trying to find the words to explain her actions. Then she turned her head towards me and boldly proclaimed, "I just don't like you." The senior manager's mouth dropped open and there was a deafening silence for what seemed like a minute. I said nothing, knowing her confession to a senior manager was proof she had violated company bias policy, which could be punished by separation. The senior manager was now pondering what next to say other than, you're fired. What I heard next was the tone of a parent speaking to a young child, counseling her that this was not the behavior we as managers should exhibit. Next the senior manager pivoted in an attempt to uncover if I had done something, so she could conclude her manager's bias was actually result of my actions, my fault. She asked why she feels that way about me. Her response was simple, "I don't know (why), I just do." So, she admitted she was doing something without being able to define why she was doing it. At this point the senior manager realized she had no defense that could help her. One might ask was her admission of not having a reason for her bias a sign of insanity or the result of some early teachings instilled by someone she relied on, someone she trusted without question. But as an adult, she couldn't point to the actual reason why she hates. This is one true experience that left a curious thought in my mind. How many people are walking around, engaging directly or indirectly with others, that really have no idea why they hate? They just do. All that is needed is an event, a sight, a person or a word to trigger an irrational, hateful response. Almost like a programmed response.

During conversations many agree that racism is used for various reasons including, but not limited to hindering and obstructing a targeted race of people from being able to achieve goals, enjoy benefits or be prosperous. It's also a means to deliver hate. So, if you are in a conversation and ask why each person uses racism you should expect to hear from some, "I don't know. I just hate you people." However, others may be able to point back to an event that impacted them personally, or indirectly through the recollections from someone else, which could be real or a figment of their imagination. For instance, I heard the recollections centered around someone being fired from their job and that person concluded it was the fault of the one African-American on staff as being the reason for them getting fired. One of the other employees concluded the African-American wasn't fired instead of the white employee because there was a quota in place that the company needed to have one minority on staff. Just one. In fact, this was a small company with less than 100 on staff and there was no government or privately funded project requiring any quotas. Do you wonder how I know this to be true? Guess who was the one African-American on staff. And I was aware there were a couple of employees who were biased against the one let go from the first day he arrived, just because he was hired as a favor to a client, plus he had negligible experience when compared to the rest on staff. In this case, I was included in the back-room conversations that were focused on convincing management he was unqualified, was a bad investment for returning a positive return on investment, and had no growth potential, at all. As the case grew wings, another shoe dropped. Rumors somehow slipped out from the finance office that alerted others of the new employee's salary being equal to, and in some cases, higher than that of more senior employees. Even though it's common for some to receive salary offers not based on experience but who they know, it still makes some people angry. In asking how the fired employee reached the conclusion to blame the one African-American employee, me, he could cite no proof, just a feeling. For me, this was an experience where I knew people didn't like this new employee and plotted against him the entire time he was there. Even still, he blamed the one black guy, and I never had participated in the plot to get him out, other than listening to the comments which incidentally, he never was given any opportunities to defend. Knowing the unsavory fruits of bias, I chose not to agree with what was spoken about the new hire during the close-door conversations about him, and didn't like it because when he was gone, I knew those involved would direct their attention to guess who. Especially since there were a few employees who had previously warned me of similar conversations focused on me when I first was hired. Lucky for me I came in with experience and quickly proved I could deliver output just like the others. And clients communicated to senior management their approval of my work. So, the lack of experience approach focused on getting rid of me wasn't initially accepted by management, given my success, but did work on the guy fired who often needed our assistance to get his assignments completed. Later, they came for me. Lucky for me I had held off the attacks long enough to have built enough seniority to warrant a hefty severance payout. I recall thinking, who would want to work for a bunch of racist anyway?

I've heard an endless number of stories in which the current flow of immigrants into a country is the reason why others can't get hired. When asking how they reached that conclusion you hear a similar response. Actually, there's no proof of any immigrants being hired into specific jobs other than very low paid jobs, which are not being sought by the group who blames them. Again, "it's just a feeling."

When thinking about individuals who don't know why they hate, I was reminded of the practice of some parents who raise their children to use racial epithets and dehumanizing practices. In addition, there's research that suggests the community in which children are raised, which may have behavioral norms being practiced, are also influences on standard biases adopted by children. If those behavioral norms include behaviors that teach the dehumanizing of one or more race of people, those children can adopt them before they have developed cognitive skills to realize they are learning racist behaviors.

Here's another personal experience that took place while I was in a southern U.S. metropolitan city. Early on one sunny Saturday morning, I was doing some shopping at a marketplace grocery store. At one point, I was pushing my shopping cart down one of those long aisles when I happen to pass a young lady who was pushing a stroller with a small toddler sitting comfortably in the stroller. As I recall, almost as if it was yesterday, there was just the three of us going in opposite directions in the aisle. As soon as I passed the woman and toddler in the stroller, I heard clear as a bell the voice of the child saying, "mommy, n'ger mommy." I immediately stopped and turned around in time to see this tiny cute girl with her arm up and index finger pointing in my direction while at the same time her little body was turned in her stroller seat looking up towards the woman pushing the stroller as if she was waiting for acknowledgement that she was accurate in what she saw and said. She was so small that I remember as I looked at her to determine her age and capability to know the meaning of what she had said, I saw those small white baby shoes you often see with the shoelaces tied together allowing you to hang the pair over your rear-view mirror. I assessed she was much too young to be aware what she had said was a historically racial epithet. After my brief assessment, I trained my eyes on the mom to see if she was going to give this little girl an acknowledgement of what she said was correct. She remained silent, ignoring the toddler, and also upon seeing my abrupt stop and turn, she avoided direct eye contact with me while I waited to hear her response. But I caught a glance where I took that moment to give my nod to communicate, I know you or someone is teaching this innocent young girl, racial epithets which as she gets older will probably result of this event imprinted on her as being a normalized racial practice and behavior. I witnessed the early results of a behavioral brainwashing of an innocent young child who at some point later in life may not be able to answer why she hates people of a particular race.

The Cold and Fatal Drink of Anxiety

There is another clear derangement in the psychological behavior of some individuals living in the United States of America that has reached what I believe to be an epidemic stage. At some point after the election of President Barack Hussein Obama, the nation's 44th President and first African-American President, holding what some believe is the most powerful political position in the world, there began an increasing number of open displays of hate that began to ooze up from the bowels of the land. Previously living just below the surface, but now having emerged so all can see. Now the level of anxiety felt by the racist who previously were hiding in plain sight had lost their control and figuratively standing on rooftops, shouting. As a result of the election, their belief in racial superiority had been shattered into little pieces. Their long-standing beliefs was proven false, and it obviously hurt them deep emotionally. Not just for a moment, but they had to endure the destruction of their faith for eight long years. By the time President Obama's second term of was over, they, the racists, had totally lost their minds. The next person who occupied the nation's seat of power was clearly a hope for the racist, that someone will restore their belief of racial superiority. However, after eight years of President Obama, their ability to make sound assessment had been skewed, damaged, and the following election quickly snapped the electorate out of their deep sleep, this is not what the country expected. Oops.

Oh well, many would ask, what could go wrong? Well racist rhetoric continued increasing without restraint. The number of hate crimes towards various groups increased while the executive leadership continued down a path to remold the country into one where hate, bullying, meanest and bigotry would be normalized. Making it easier for believers of hate to come to the forefront, out of the darkness, and begin to stand boldly in front of cameras to proclaim their beliefs and values with the hope of recruiting followers. And they did. They were successful in raising the level of anxiety to a point where violence followed. Mass shootings increased. The vision of children, students, adults, babies, senior citizens and people sharing fellowship within their place of worship, all began to be shot to death as a result of the anxiety built up within the minds of hate-mongers. Did they even know why one day they would decide to load a magazine filled with bullets into their military assault weapons and then casually enter a high school to kill students trying to learn, or to enter an A.M.E. church, a Synagogue or a Baptist church to shoot worshipers? Did they know why they decided to mail bombs to elected politicians or what's driving them to attack the messenger also known as the national media? Did they know why they drove down a crowded street to run over people who were protesting hate? Was the anxiety so great that they couldn't bare the words that provoked their anger and so they had to act beyond just hearing the hate speeches that embraced all their fears of losing control, traditions, jobs, privileges, favoritism, purity and most of all, power? They couldn't take it any longer. Something had to give. Well, most people can conclude something encouraged them to drink from the goblet of fire, a cold chalice filled with anxiety, and off they went to display their allegiance and conviction to their leaders of hate. Words are powerful. Growing up in communities where hate has been normalized is impactful to those who have not reached the age where they can fully understand the consequences of their actions. For toddlers and young children, they haven't developed enough cognitive skills to recognized the hypnotic spell delivered in hate speech. And so, as anxiety increases and individuals increase their displays of anger, and the epidemic eats into the minds of decent people, the number of mass shootings continue with more frequency. The voices of psychologists seem to have been muzzled resulting in a deafening silence, almost as if they are unsure just how much their role is sorely needed. Watching as the epidemic widens, without constraints, without corrective messaging from those who know the cause.

Gun violence. Mailed bombs. Motor vehicles used as weapons. Physical fights. Unable to understand the consequences of their actions until some point around the age of twenty-five. That leaves a lot of opportunities to convert someone into being a hate-monger. With the advancement of social media technology and propaganda now unchained, the hate-mongers are free to seek out and find the minds that are not trained with the shield of cognitive skills. Unable to really understand why violence is being considered as an option? To be able to use reasoning to think about what will be the result of their actions? To recognize anxiety and fear are emotions that leaders throughout time have come to realize and advised us are emotions each person must overcome. They are the obstacles on the game board that you have to eliminate in-order to proceed with the game. In this case, the game is for life.

While reflecting on these events I suspect some people could easily conclude these actions by the racially-biased manager, the innocent little toddler and the teen-ager packing a military assault rifle were the results of brainwashing that will require psychological counseling and behavior modification to resolve. But if we take this discussion further it is really difficult to conclude what are the specific states of mind that motivates an adult to engage in actions that are hurtful to others. However, for discussion purposes, we can ask individuals what are their foundational beliefs and possibly why they are important. If we objectively think about why you believe in something, we should be able to narrow down that each of your beliefs provides some type of gratification in the form of a psychological reward, either tangible or intangible. Those rewards fortify your conviction to those beliefs.

Gratifying rewards might fall into various categories. Obvious ones would be having confidence and reliance on a higher spiritual power for your fulfillment, feeling loved, receiving a sense of belonging to a group, achieving a high level of notoriety, gaining financial success, feeling you have power and authority, having a sense of safety, being able to maintain good health, and one of the most powerful rewards would be receiving acknowledgement from parents, peer or mentors.

Should we also consider the age of the individual when considering what might be gratifying to them? Most people would agree as we age our needs often change. According to Professor Abraham Maslow's psychological hierarchy of humanistic needs, we each have various needs related to our physiological requirements, needs for safety, love and belonging, esteem and self-actualization. When having a discussion on racism it would make sense to try to understand what are an individual's strongest needs. Those needs could be influenced by the type of community where one lives. Or their social development and level of involvement with popular groups that could influence how well they were liked while attending high school.

I also heard a noted psychiatrist, Dr. Carl Bell, speaking on a popular radio program about irrational behaviors often done by youth.

He noted there are findings in national research that concluded the human brain doesn't develop the capacity to be rational or understand the consequences of one's actions until the mid-twenties. Based on this research it would be easy to understand why someone in their younger years may not be able to explain why they participate in dehumanizing practices targeting specific races. They just do. At that stage of their mental development they may not really understand the repercussions of violent hate crimes until after they have been arrested for their crime, and locked up long enough for their brains to mature. This might also shed some light on why they initially joined hate groups, neighborhood gangs or social media groups that gives participants a sense of purpose, belonging or a sense they will become empowered through participation. I think parents who teach their kids to hate could be sealing their fate to live out their lives in jail. All being done while their children are in their formative years and before they have the mental capacity to understand the consequences of their actions.

Chapter Three: Implicit Bias, The Inception

When I've been in conversations about implicit bias the discussion often centers around events where one or more participants have been negatively impacted. Discussions also focus on areas where some realize they actually have implicit bias towards others. During these conversations participants tend to be reluctant to admit they have bias towards others until it becomes clear that we all have them. But it only becomes an issue when our bias becomes hurtful to others or blocks a specific race of people from receiving fair treatment.

The Merriam-Webster Dictionary defines bias to be a personal and sometimes unreasoned judgment, prejudice or an inclination of outlook or temperament.

The Merriam-Webster Dictionary defines implicit to be something that is capable of being understood from something unexpressed or not revealed.

So, an implicit bias would be an unexpressed, not revealed, unreasoned judgement, prejudice of inclination of outlook or temperament.

To get everyone on the same page, I think most would agree they are inclined to believe kids of a certain age are not able to make good decisions. But when you think about the process needed to make good decisions most would agree you will need sound information along with cognitive skills. If you provided sound and accurate information to kids who have developed some cognitive skills, they might be able to make some good decisions. We all experience this as our parents gain trust and gradually begin to remove their direct supervision. However, if you decide kids of a certain race will never make good decisions you might decide they should be severely punished or incarcerated after making a bad decision. This would hinder their opportunities be nurtured, receive sound and accurate information and learn from their mistakes while still in a healthy environment. This example of implicit bias explains why children belonging to a specific race are often treated as though they are adults after arrested for making the mistake of breaking a law. It also explains why they are sentenced to incarceration instead of probation with supervised counseling, which could allow them the opportunity to learn and change their behavior before they actually become adults.

While participating in conversations on implicit bias I often like to share one experience I had during a time when I was selected to be on a jury for a municipal criminal court case. During the trial, testimony was presented against the accused teenagers, that the arresting officers noticed the smell of weed (marijuana) around them at the time when they were arrested. During our jury deliberations an elderly man said he was going to vote guilty because he believed anyone who smoked weed would probably do anything. When asked if he had ever smoked weed or gotten high when he was younger, his response was no. I began to wonder if his generalization was based on some 'wacky weed' paranoia. Immediately upon hearing his response others began to challenge his reasoning. One juror asked, "Well how would you know what someone will do, and where was there any testimony regarding the specific behavior of the teenagers?" Another juror spoke up to remind us that cigarette smokers usually retain the smell of cigarette smoke on their clothes long after they actually smoked a cigarette. Having agreed with that statement, another juror asked, "how can we know when these teenagers smoked weed, or if they were just in the presence of someone who was smoking, and as result might have been exposed to second-hand smoke?" Despite this input the elderly man shouted out, "I don't care, I believe when you smoke weed you are going to do some type of mischief." His bias was extremely entrenched and could result in jail time for these teenagers. I began to wonder, was he biased against these two teenagers because he believed everyone who smokes weed will be driven to be involved with criminal activities, or was he biased because these teenagers were members of a race that was different than his? Throughout our deliberations he became further withdrawn, only to periodically vocalize he had made his decision and was not changing no matter what others presented. In this case, his bias was more important than the logic presented by fellow jurors.

How do you think implicit bias develops in the minds of individuals? In an academic paper written by Dr. Erin Winkler, she points to various psychological research that suggests children at six months of age are capable of non-verbally recognizing unfamiliar faces, including those of a different race and gender. In addition, toddlers between the ages of three-to-five years of age develop racial biases based on the information they have gathered from various environmental sources in addition to influences from parents. This means their biases could potentially align to some that are totally separate from their parent's beliefs. The research also suggests the children seem to pick up subtle influences that could include a sense of privilege if they perceive they actually belong to a specific social group in the area where they live. This means if there are normalized practices like what might be aligned to specific geographic regions and communities, the children might align to those practices.

This research now presents a challenge to parents to be more mindful of the places they go that could leave a bad impression on their children and as result might require impartial guidance for their children who have yet to develop cognitive skills. They are potentially absorbing the sights, sounds and interactions of people each place they are exposed.

If you took your kids to a sports event where there was cheering, booing, yelling, anger displayed towards other teams or referees, the crowd shouting for violence, to hit or smash somebody, the children could potentially assume those behaviors to be normal. If they were with you when you went to a political event, they could easily adopt behaviors that take place at those events. Common experiences at political events might include yelling, language and words focused on blaming one candidate for problems in life, name calling, propaganda, defamation of character, bullying, inciting violence against challengers and their supporters or delivering hate speeches. When you assess the number of character traits you might experience at political events, rarely will you hear words that complement the challengers. The majority of what you will hear is focused on encouraging voters to dislike opposing candidates. For some they will hold on to a sentiment long after the elections have concluded. If you want your children to learn about dignity, respect and common decency it's possible, but probably will not happen at political events. If the child has not reached their mid-twenties, they could easily begin to believe the actions witnessed at political events are normal. If they were taken with their parents each Sunday to religious or faith-based services, it's possible they might be surrounded by positive messages, joyous singing, praising God or a higher power aligned to their beliefs, fellowship with people from their community, acts of charity, laughter, lots of food and smiles. As a result, they may grow up considering a number of positive values as being a norm in their environment.

I recall as a very young child I had the experience of travelling across country by train, almost every year when my mom would take us to visit her family. By the time I was a senior in high school, I had decided to be a locomotive engineer and travel across the country. It was the exposure to traveling by train as a young child that was just fascinating and provided a treasure of experiences. It was enjoyable, exciting, and I met children on the train who enjoyed running from car to car and up to the observation car, just as I did. And when I sat in the observation car, which I perceived as a glassed-in bubble on top of one car, I could sit back and watch from the top of the train, looking forward and backwards as each car snaked around curves, through tunnels and over bridges. It was a care-free experience where I found people of different races, all riding along together, and some who would say hi and tell me their stories. I remember feeling sad when some of the kids I met would exit at a stop, and they waved good-by. I became fascinated by seeing the huge locomotive engines, the sound of their powerful engines and the speed we travelled across country, often though the backyards of family homes. I saw America along with the different faces and the different communities. I gained a first-hand education about diversity that could not be taught in schools. This was my vision of enjoying a happy life while making a living. Unfortunately, when it was time for me to go off to college, I was unable to find a degree program for learning about being a locomotive engineer. So, I settled for continuing my studies in music and technology, focused on becoming a creative technologist, capable of doing one, both or a combination of the two.

In the absence of adult nurturing and guidance, young children who are relying on adult supervision until their cognitive abilities develop, may become challenged with sorting out their biases upon initial recognition of skin color and gender. And so, you may initially see the biases of children emerge at a very young age through their decisions of who they choose to play with or exclude from their play group, based on skin color and gender. Over time they will build upon their early biases unless there is guidance to help them develop into individuals with racial socialization skills, multi-cultural awareness, acknowledging their own race and traditions while having respect for people of other races. They'll require encouragement to avoid racial, gender and class bias. They'll need help with understanding human decency and civility.

For individuals belonging to groups being targeted for racism, their parents often realize they need to provide guidance to their children on how to navigate in an environment that may be unfair and hostile to them. Some groups call this "The Talk." The details of "The Talk" is customized based on the level of normalization of racial bias that may exist in their community. However, this training comes with the risk of developing additional types of racial biases since children may choose either to be confrontational or passive when engaging individuals of a different race who are unfair, disrespectful or engaged with dehumanizing behavior.

The conversation on how racial biases initiates introduces another topic for discussion. What are options to provide implicit bias counseling for those toddlers, children, teens and young adults who grow up without a psychologically stable and cognizant adult in their lives?

Below are some implicit bias influencers.
The Beginning
1. Parents and family members.
2. All of the surroundings and people the toddler experiences.

3. Babysitters.
4. Daycare.
5. Nursery school.
6. Friends / Peer.
7. Faith-based education / religion / humane principles.
8. Normalized community or adopted practices.
9. Media messaging – owner's vision; social; general market.
10. Propaganda – primarily orchestrated; secondary.
11. An impactful event.
12. Being segregated from factual information.

Possible Obstacles
1. Concern for potential reputational risk (personal; political; business).
2. Concern for potential economic risk – fear of rejection, isolation.
3. Dedication to maintaining traditional practices.
4. Teachers / Guidance counselors – formal; informal.
5. Generational avoidance, continuing a pattern & practice of not engaging in any discussions due to fear of potential confrontational conflicts (physical or verbal), or economic and reputational risk.
    a. Increased confrontation with those accustomed to long-standing traditions or cultural practices.
    b. Growing support for those having strong desire to change tradition, be treated fairly and to evolve.
6. Internal and external tribal reputation / peer pressure
    a. Sympathetic.
    b. Non-conforming.

7. Sense of entitlement, superiority, caste, economic status, level of education.

The Path to Diminishing Personal Biases
1. Acknowledgment and acceptance that we all have bias, but some impact the health, prosperity and the safety of others. Through awareness, conflicts might be avoided.
2. Witnessing what appears to be an unjust act or pattern of unjust actions motivates activism, personal involvement with corrective actions, overtly or anonymously.
3. Faith or religious principles.
4. Community or adopted practices.
5. Media messaging – owner's vision; social media; general market.
6. A positive experience.
7. Being exposed to factual information.

Two sources of Anxiety created by Bias

If you happen to find you are in a conversation about racism, I urge you to ask others what they believe are some institutions or practices that create anxiety. I found there are a couple of areas that are consistently brought up as provoking anxiety. Of course, each person will have some that impact them based on their own unique personalities and psychological needs. But when you take a look at news coverage around the world, there are some areas that seem to be continually in the news and impact individuals no matter their race. The areas people bring up as resulting in anxiety have been consistently related to jobs and what are perceived to be biased methods the law enforcement and judicial systems utilize when interacting with the communities they are sworn to protect and serve.

No matter where you look, people are always talking about jobs. Whether it's the need for creating more jobs, job loss, blaming immigrants for making it difficult to obtain jobs, how to find a job and there's extreme bias expressed about who is the first or only ones hired for available jobs. In some countries there are mass protests, heated elections, military coups and violence. One of the controversial points of focus centers on the consistent use of implicit bias by some hiring managers. In some countries there are laws prohibiting bias being practiced in the hiring process and workplace, but there is rarely any enforcement of those laws, and so it continues unbridled. As a result of bias some organizations have one race consistently selected to fill executive and senior leadership roles. In addition, that same bias is spread throughout the decision processes utilized when determining who will be selected to fill other roles. This internal bias within employment practices can also contribute to reinforcing the fears of those who believe there is a diminishing number of available jobs due to an influx of immigrants. Although there continues to be various social-economic challenges that hinder job creation, bias within the hiring process also contributes to distinct segments in the available pool of applicants not receiving consideration, resulting in low employment for them. For those who begin to gain more cultural awareness, increase their interactions with individuals belonging to various race groups, they may adjust their thinking regarding their fears of, and discomfort with being around individuals of other races. As a result, we should expect to see a more diverse workforce and less racial bias used within the employment practices. As more individuals move into the workforce, the fear of immigrants taking all of the available jobs should decrease.

The other anxiety area highlighted in conversations focuses around implicit bias and racial profiling utilized by law enforcement systems when interacting with one or more segments of the communities they are sworn to protect and serve. In some regions implicit bias and racial profiling seems to be a traditional practice within law enforcement and judicial systems. At times it might seem as though these two systems are aligned worldwide in using the same philosophies with how to interact with the communities they are sworn to serve and protect. As new psychological research is gathered in the areas of implicit bias and racial profiling, the research continues to confirm that distinct race groups are being unfairly impacted. As a result, more organizations are beginning to include training to help individuals realize biases that they were previously unaware. After completing implicit bias training some law enforcement employees who were initially resistant to the idea of them being biased towards specific races, have become more knowledgeable and believe over time the training will facilitate a change in their behavior. However, since the research is still new, the practice of racial profiling and implicit bias is still widespread. Those in leadership roles have not realized the value of including this type of training for their resources.

Implicit bias is also a challenge for business leaders as they struggle with the need to diversify their workforce for businesses whose goals are to increase their market share internationally. Knowing their business growth and long-term viability is threatened if their market share only includes one segment of the population while their competition expands across multiple segments of the market including international markets, their only option is to diversify their workforce. They must build a diverse workforce, gain multi-cultural awareness, add socialization and language skills and minimize fears related to interacting with various races. This is not an easy task, but one they know they will need to undertake or lose their business. This also means corporations will need to become increasingly involved with race relations in the regions where they provide products and services.

Chapter Four: You Can Run, but You Can't Hide, from History

There's a traditional defense that is centered on using the past as an alibi. In verbal exchanges someone will say "I had nothing to do with what happened in the past." That defense normally evokes emotional responses like one of the following: "If that's the case, why are you still using the same patterns and practices used in the past, today?" "Why do you vote for politicians who support racist policies?" "Why do you directly or indirectly support racist practices at work or in your community?" "Why do you say nothing when you witness racist practices, patterns, policies and behaviors?" "Why do you prefer following print and media communication channels that deliver dishonest, unfair coverage, reinforce racist generalizations, provide discussions focused on dividing members of the population by race, disseminating disinformation and hurtful statements concerning targeted racial groups?" Any of these questions might be followed with a slew of evidence that bring attention to unfair hiring and promotion practices in the workplace, politicians maintaining 'Jim Crow' laws or sentencing disparities resulting in one race incarcerated at a higher rate than others. They might also point to statistics showing that judicial probation decisions are being given out to one race more than another or pointing out each instance where police behavior resembles the behavior of the slave patrols of the past. The list of evidence could continue with discussions around the various practices used to ensure an imbalance of wealth, power, economic resources and access to public benefits. There are discrimination practices like racial profiling, redlining, higher loan requirements for individuals who have excellent credit scores. There is unequal funding of public education, public funds not allocated for community infrastructure investment and a lack of adequate healthcare support being made available. This is where the facts just don't support the rhetoric of having nothing to do with the past. Each day you are adding events to the past. Upon faced with reality, participants may retreat into avoidance instead of acknowledgement. However, in some cases the conversation begins to consider solutions where individuals can comfortably become active standing up against or just avoiding direct and indirect participation in racist patterns and practices for the good of their community. Unfortunately, before jumping on-board to enact change, some individuals may need to weigh potential negative impacts to their individual reputations among their peer and community. In addition, there could be negative impacts to family members. However, some might conclude the best solution for them will be to participate behind the scenes, privately with actions to minimize racist behaviors.

Although some seem to prefer not to acknowledge or read about documented race-related events that took place, you can always be assured that those families that were targeted, will not forget. They will pass on recollections from generation to generation as lessons learned and to motivate the next generation to proactively engage in strategies that will protect them from the recurrence of racist behaviors. For those who read history it becomes easy to identify racist behaviors that are the same, or similar to those events documented in the past. As a result, each day another page of documented evidence is added into the book of racism.

The inference that you had nothing to do with what happened in the past presents an argument that may be philosophically implausible when considering the possibility that yesterday, you might have participated directly or indirectly in racist behaviors that were documented into the book. You have added to documented history of racism. And then there's today. Will you be adding another page? Well then, you just can't hide from history. Each day, you become a part of it. Hmm. As baby-boomers might say, "that's deep."

Throughout history there have been continual political debates centered on the control of land, power, wealth and jobs. Those conversations rarely exist without the inclusion of immigration and refugee policies designed to limit benefits moving from one group to another. In the United States of America, the original inhabitants of this country belonged to various American Indian nations. However, immigrants escaping harmful practices in their countries, began arriving from various European countries and eventually began to claim the country as their own. Each new group of immigrants, hoping to have exclusivity over the land, natural resources and potential wealth opportunities began to create policies to implement a toll-gate that controlled who could come into the country they falsely claimed as their own. Borders were constructed around territories and armed militia was put in place to reinforce each new immigration policy. Unbridled border crossing payment structures were implemented. Preferred status became a requirement for entry into some territories. And if an area was discovered to have an abundance of natural resources, like gold, oil or high economic growth potential, only those having military, political or economic support were able to enter to reap benefits.

Key foundational characteristics that remain true to immigration policies include the coveting of potential wealth opportunities, ensuring the purity of a race and culture and making sure natural resources are restricted to use by only a few. Also included was the need to ensure the safety of those living within borders and the ability to implement rules, policies and practices that will maintain the lifestyle of the inhabitants within the boundaries.

In many conversations centered on immigration policies we often hear coded messaging communicated directly to one group as if no one else can decipher the messaging. They believe the coded message will allow them deniability of their true support of restrictive policies. Knowing they are doing something wrong, so they seek to hide their actions. At times the messaging is centered on raising fear that you will lose your current way of life or immigrants are to blame for whatever is negative in your life. Sometimes the message proclaims your property values will lower if others enter within the borders. Other messages are constructed to raise fear that those from another race will take all of the currently available employment opportunities. Not once considering people from their own race will be fighting internally, within existing borders, for employment opportunities. There is also the concern that existing racial and cultural values will be diluted or totally lost. You may also hear a concern communicated that you will see an increase in crime, impacting the safety of those living within the designed borders.

Overall, the coded messaging targets a fear that any change to existing policies, practices and laws will remove protections over the favoritism that allowed the flow of benefits going mostly to one group. As you might imagine if you were a member of a group that was the first to usurp control over a land full of natural resources that resulted in your wealth, I'm sure you would fight with every tool you could find to help you maintain your lifestyle. Understood. However, those messages exclude the reality that more benefits will continue to be created based on supply and demand. But when that fight to avoid change results in harm to others you can expect those harmed will seek ways to eliminate each activity that has brought them harm. Each harmful event resulting in an inverse equalizing event. Kind of like Newton's Third Law.

In conversations it's often brought up that current residents and citizens of a country somehow collectively overlook they were immigrants or refugees while overlooking the original inhabitants. Rarely honoring the ones who nurtured the land into a viable location where now so many find value. You will hear, "wait a minute, how are you concerned about immigrants when your family were immigrants?"

American Indian Nations

In the United States of America, it was various American Indian nations that nurtured the land and yet few of the current residents acknowledge them, honor them, respect them or give them a fair share of the resources they nurtured and protected. Is it naïve to ignore that many continue to immigrate into the United States from around the world to enjoy the vast and extraordinary benefits that continue to exist and flourish? We owe the indigenous people worldwide a debt that cannot be repaid. And we can acknowledge and honor them.

Now, I have a topic for discussion I'd like to bring before you for our on-gong conversation. I can understand why for generation after generation, some white Americans support racism and to have a disdain for African-Americans, seeing that they might blame the African slaves for many of their families falling into severe financial difficulties and turmoil as the institution of slavery was dismantled. Afterall, how could those slaves turn their backs on their owners and choose not to remain, working for free and enjoying such a great and enjoyable life. So, the blame aspect is a bit skewed (it was actually members of their own race who created the financial collapse) but somewhat understandable when you think about losing free labor and no one to do the physical work. So, I understand the hatred towards African-Americans being passed on by each generation. But why is this happening to the American Indians? The indigenous people and original owners of all the land, natural resources and potential wealth opportunities. Why are they still treated in such a harsh manner? Still being treated poorly, dehumanized and not recognized by the current nation's leaders for their contributions? **No national holiday to honor them, not one**? What did they do to deserve a continual sentence and the target of racist patterns and practices? Many of whom still live within internment camp reservations and are struggling for adequate healthcare. Can someone please respond to enlighten me?

My response. No one seems to care enough to ask the nation's leaders, why this practice continues. Has this part of history become a normality for so many descendants of immigrants because they have chosen to ignore history? Have they become immune to their own experiences where their race was once the target of racial patterns, practices, generalizations and hurtful epithets? If asked, I suspect the answer might be, "I don't know."

I'm going to say, yes, we should acknowledge the past and show some respect for the people who nurtured the land that others now enjoy and call their home. The same respect you have when a family member bequest their property and possessions to surviving family members. I hope others will not forget the true reason why today's descendants of immigrants value their new spot of land so much. It was a collective but diverse set of policies, practices and actions by the indigenous people, the non-immigrants that resulted in sustained value.

Going forward the descendants of immigrants have the capability to be aware of the historically recurring racist patterns and practices, and not to continue them in the present. Through awareness you can establish a mindset to implement actions that will result in the continual practice to nurture and flourish existing value not just for a few, but for many.

Chapter Five: Our Private Discussion

Q1: History has documented a number of cases where the original indigenous people of a geographic region were forced off their land by colonizers and later by immigrants, both originating from foreign lands. In some cases, colonizers and immigrants began to claim land and resources owned and occupied by the indigenous people by using unfair treaties, military action, embargoes that cut the inhabitants off from sacred burial grounds, natural resources like fertile farm land, water, hunting & fishing, oil fields and mineral deposits. Over time as colonizers began to increase the limitation for access to man-made resources like trading posts (stores) with fresh food, supplies, medical assistance and implemented laws that gave advantages to one group over another, the original inhabitants resisted, resulting in the colonizers needing armed groups of individuals to ensure the colonizers could retain all their spoils. With armed groups came violence up to and including murder. What do you think were some central factors why the original inhabitants were treated so unfairly? Why do you think many of these practices still continue against the original inhabitants?

Q2: Raising children requires continual input and guidance from their parents and adults in their lives. Why do you think some parents teach their children behaviors and words that are publicly known to be associated with racism? For example, why do parents teach their kids not to trust people belonging to a specific racial group, to stay away from them and to treat them unfairly? Do you think these parents consider at some point their children could realize their parents taught them to hate their friends and as a result have at an early stage, planted a seed that could impact their relationship with their children later in life?

Q3: How do you feel when people belonging to a racial group **different than your own**, begin to strongly express their lack of tolerance for some actions by people belonging to **your** own racial group?

Q4: How do you feel when people belonging to **your own** racial group begin to strongly express their lack of tolerance against the complaints or actions coming from another group?

Q5: What would you say is the difference between Q3 and Q4?

Q6: Where is the Trail of Tears?

Q7: How did Thomas Dartmouth "Daddy" Rice become famous?

Q8: What is the purpose of the fictional Star Trek's StarFleet General Order One, also known as the "prime directive?" Do you know the name of the notable organization that supports similar principles whose name was coined by U.S. President Franklin Delano Roosevelt in 1942 and officially established in 1945?

Q9: What was the land solution implemented by Europeans in the United States of America, Canada and Australia for the Australian Aboriginals and the North American Indians? It starts with a 'R'.

Q10: Do you believe rural communities are safer than suburban communities? If so, can you list reasons? Do you believe suburban communities are safer than urban communities? If so, can you list reasons? Since people who formerly were residents living in urban communities often move to the suburbs and some later move to rural communities, how does that impact your original list of reasons?

Q11: Why do you think racist organizations support specific candidates?

Q12: Most people would conclude at some point it becomes common knowledge that there are specific patterns and practices that are determined by those targeted, to be racist. At that point it would be difficult for an individual not to be aware of actions known to be disrespectful, dehumanizing, unfair and hurtful to a specific race of people. Upon having that awareness, whether you agree or not about the action being characterized as being racist, how do you feel when people close to you, let you know in private conversations, they are proponents of practices characterized as being racist, but in public they present a different character? Have you ever spoke in favor of racist behaviors in private but realize your statements could result in negative impacts to you if you communicated the same statements in public?

Q13: How would you feel if one of the most influential persons in your life compelled you to adopt or support clearly racist patterns or practices?

Q14: If you were asked to interview candidates to be hired for an open employment opportunity and the one who most impressed you was a member of a race that was being regularly ostracized with negative generalizations, would you skip over to the next person to avoid having to defend against the possibility of you receiving negative criticism?

Q15: Have you ever expressed dismay upon witnessing a member of a racial group other than your own, displaying academic, professional, managerial or communication capabilities beyond your expectations? Some expressions of dismay might be: you're different from others (in your race); you speak differently than others (in your race); I'm surprised you know about matters such as this or know how to do this; I'm surprised you've been so successful; Did you actually graduate from college (or only enrolled and never completed)?

Q16: Have you ever felt the need to provide a disclaimer to your friends or associates for your association with someone of a different race? You might present the disclaimer by telling them (not to worry) he or she (who is a member of a different race than yours) is ok. What about your friends or associates led you to believe you needed to provide a disclaimer?

Q17: Do you ever feel things are getting out of control as you see more racial groups publicly protesting about being mistreated? Would you feel better if they protested differently but not publicly? Do you feel there is a proper time and place for protests? Do you wish you could turn back the clock and go back to the days of law and order where people of certain races were kept in their place? Have you heard people from older generations proclaim back in the day they got along with the same people who are now protesting?

Q18: Do you feel you have substantial cultural awareness from a global perspective? If not, do you have any fear that your limited knowledge of cultural awareness could create problems for you at some point? Have you ever taken time to do an internet search on historically documented racist activities so that you can become more knowledgeable of actions that are dehumanizing and hurtful to specific races around the world?

Q19: Would you prefer to vote for a candidate who runs on a platform focused on increased law and order which to many equates to stiffer patrolling of minorities? Would you prefer to vote for a candidate who runs on a platform focused on working to ensure there is fair use of policing authority?

Q20: Have you ever thought about what might be the reasons protestors are arrested and how fair are the laws used to arrest them?

Q21: Do you think whistle-blowers are treated in similar ways as protestors? In some countries there are laws to protect whistle-blowers from being harassed, threatened and punished by those they identify as causing harm to communities and public safety. Should laws re-classify protestors as being whistle-blowers who are focused on identifying people who are causing harm to a specific race of people and negatively impacting their safety?

Q22: Have you ever wondered what were the specific laws Dr. Martin Luther King Jr. or Nelson Mandela broke in their respective countries that resulted in their arrests? Are you a bit curious enough to check the internet so you can become knowledgeable of the specific laws used for their arrests?

Q23: Are there laws in your area or country that require you to obtain approval from authorities before you can protest something in public? Are there laws in your area or country that define acceptable ways which you will be allowed to protest or express your opinions? Are there laws in your area or country that prohibit you from meeting privately to discuss plans to protest something?

Q24: If you were a member of a group that has been the consistent target of racist practices and your group began to gain power, would you be in favor of supporting legislation to increase the punishment for individuals found guilty of practicing racism with the hope of encouraging others to avoid racists behaviors?

Q25: As a result of the damage fascism and extremist hate practices did to its population, Germany passed laws that restricts hate speeches and expressions of hate. It is illegal to produce, distribute or display symbols from the Nazi era. In addition, Holocaust denial is illegal. Anybody who dehumanizes an individual or a group based on their race or religion, or anybody who tries to instigate hate or promotes violence against a group or an individual, could face imprisonment. Although it's difficult to legislate thought and beliefs, these measures were implemented to modify the behavior of their population and facilitate healthy socialization. Without these measures do you think individuals will change on their own? Should other countries enact similar legislation?

Q26: If you were a member of a racial group identified as one that has used racism to maintain your traditions and control of power, but began to lose power over those you've targeted, do you worry about potential repercussions as a result of the pain and mistreatment some in your race have caused?

Q27: The populations of many continents have experienced racism. Groups living in Europe, Asia, Oceania, Africa, North and South America have documented the various race groups that have been the targets of racism. Since racism is not limited to one country or race of people have you ever considered what is the fundamental value of racism that allows it to exist so widely? If racism was no longer practiced, do you believe that would utterly destroy people or stop them from reaching their goals?

Q28: Do you think countries should include training about racism as part of their standard education programs? Should there be coordinated lessons that involve one or both parents?

Q29: If you are a member of a group that is the target of racism, have you participated in groups focused on developing and then communicating options that can mitigate negative impacts to you and your family?

Q30: Have you ever felt enough anxiety, fear or hate that you believe violence against a specific group will resolve your anxiety, fear or hate? If so, knowing violence would be a criminal act that can potentially result in your imprisonment or death, have you sought out assistance from a professional specialist before committing criminal activities? If not, why not?

Q31: Knowing that racism is embedded within various cultures around the world do you believe there is a place you could go to escape it? Do you believe if one racial group were removed from your area, everything in life would be better for you? Do you believe some or most of the problems you have would go away?

Q32: Do you believe the nature of racism is so ingrained in our minds, cultures, and so highly reinforced by environmental influences worldwide that everyone will experience it sooner or later?

Q33: Do you feel racism is so ingrained in various cultures that you will never be able to achieve goals and prosperity for yourself or your family?

Q34: Parents are usually the most influential adults in their children's lives. Newton's third law of physics states for every action there is an equal but opposite reaction. Do you think it will be more valuable to teach children to initiate hate towards one or more race, or teach them to reciprocate mutually to those who initiate racism towards them?

Q35: Do you feel the way things are going in the area where you live that you and your family will probably benefit from the institution of racism throughout your entire life?

Q36: What is your suggestion for addressing racism if you are the target of racist patterns and practices? What is your suggestion for those who are supporting racism directly or indirectly?

Chapter Six: Conclusion

Will racism ever be eradicated from society? Possibly not for a long time. Is there a cure for racism? Yes, but to obtain the cure you will need to have an enlightenment of humanistic thinking and develop a highly disciplined mind. You'll need a purging of hate and the awakening of the spiritual mind. Expunging of dehumanizing behaviors and beliefs from within while adopting more of the highest agape love for humanity and each other. This is not a new recommendation but foundational principles to develop one's character that has been taught throughout history, in many languages, in many philosophies, in many world religions, but rarely fully adopted. Those who seek this higher thought path can achieve enlightenment within their lifetime. To successfully navigate past the various obstacles and challenges on this path, it will require having a true desire to respect the customs and traditions of others as long as they don't result in harm to you or your family. You will need to be mentally capable to humble yourself and then acknowledge your own lack of knowledge could result in you doing something that could be labeled as being racist. That would require the strength and confidence in one's self to seek forgiveness for any harm done, and possibly a recompense given for any loss you caused. This step alone will prevent many from continuing on the higher thought path. The acknowledgement of recognizing your own lack of knowledge when it comes to multi-cultural awareness includes the awareness that it is virtually impossible to know how each interaction with individuals from other races could be hurtful or disrespectful to their customs or beliefs. However, that acknowledgement should encourage you to take steps to gain multi-cultural awareness. And in the absence of the same, you should begin to approach interactions with all individuals with respect and an openness to seeking mutually respectable interactions. With these steps you will become a wiser and more enlightened person just through your acknowledgement alone. Upon initiating your daily quest to gain multicultural awareness on a global scale, you should want to become proactive in practices that oppose known racist behaviors. In some cases, it may be appropriate to issue an apology for giving anyone pain or disrespect. This is another difficult step to move further away from being classified as being a racist as a result of your lack of knowledge or understanding. These are steps to enlightening and disciplining your mind and thoughts, reinforced by actions. A wise man called James, an Apostle of Jesus The Christ taught, "a man is justified by works, and not by faith only." "Faith without works is dead." If you have belief in something, conviction and are committed to enlightening your mind to eradicate racism from your thoughts and deeds, it only makes sense that you should want to do something that supports your beliefs.

Shame, Guilt and Pain

In many of the conversations regarding racism I've heard individuals acknowledge that their family history included individuals who were slaves. However, I've never heard anyone acknowledge they had someone in their family that were slave owners, or had a history of doing harm to others. I don't expect to hear anyone admit their great grandfather murdered slaves by hanging them, or shot American Indians in the act of taking the land that was later passed down through family inheritance, but you have to conclude the grandchildren of murderers are walking among us. For most decent people there's shame and possibly a sense of transferred guilt associated with that acknowledgement. That type of acknowledgement could also come with a fear of repercussions even though I don't believe the children or great grandchildren should be punished for the crimes of their parents or great grandparents. But the fear of repercussions, guilt and shame will forever be documented as one of the family secrets that could motivate a deep seeded desire for added security and segregation. However, many of us face emotional crossroads throughout our lives that include shame, guilt or pain.

I've heard health professionals and counselors recommend the process for healing and recovery includes acknowledgement, forgiving others who have caused pain and having the strength to apologize. Many have learned the ability to apologize for harm they've caused is not weakness, but takes confidence in yourself. An enlightenment of knowing you are strong enough to be proactive in healing yourself and others. These are the doorways of enlightenment that are difficult to complete and for many they shall not pass. It is a tremendous emotional hurdle to achieve a purging of shame, guilt and pain from the hallways of our minds. Most will carry throughout their lives all types of baggage resulting from the pain received from one or more experience. Standing at the doorways while simultaneously working through healing.

I've heard the voices of those who forgave mass shooters, the voices of family members and who apologized for the actions done by a family member or the harm they have personally caused to a family. I've heard political leaders apologize for atrocities done by their countries in the past. I've seen individuals volunteer as ways to offer recompense for personal transgressions or for societal impacts to segments of their communities. These are the true diamonds in our world, actively working to heal and strengthen their selves, others or correct the transgressions done by others whom they may not know personally. They have boldly walked through the doorways and towards enlightenment. They provide examples for all to watch, learn and imitate.

Are you able to acknowledge the pain created by yourself or your ancestors? Are you able to forgive others for transgressions done against you or your family? Are you able to apologize for harm that you personally caused or was done by ancestors? I've heard many say they had nothing to do with what their ancestors may have done. And that's true, but does that mean you should do nothing to reverse the harm that may still exist in your community? Does that mean you should look the other way when you see racist behaviors or continue to participate in racist behaviors? I would think all decent humanistic people would want to remove harm. To purge shame, guilt and pain from everywhere it exists. These are some of the most difficult challenges for curing racism. The path for those who participate in racist behaviors and the path for those who have been the targets. The doorways through which many shall not pass, but it can be done.

At this point you should begin to assess just how steep of a climb it will be for you to obtain the cure for racism. What are the steps you can achieve? What are the steps you will need to work on? Can you acknowledge your lack of knowledge of cultural awareness on a global scale? Do you have a true desire to respect the customs and traditions of others as long as they don't result in harm to you or your family? Do you have the strength and character to offer an apology for giving anyone pain or disrespect? Have you proactively initiated actions (works) that are focused on opposing and eradicating known racist behaviors? They might be direct or indirect, public or anonymous actions.

Is it possible that many of us have made racist statements, participated in racist behaviors adopted by family, friends, workplace associates or become desensitized to the harm inflicted by generational actions associated with racism? I believe so. I believe many individuals have probably knowingly or unknowingly made racist statements, supported racist practices or looked the other way and remained silent after recognizing a hurtful act done by others. I believe most people know when they are doing something hurtful to others or doing something that will negatively impact a specific race. Even children know when they have done something wrong. It's something that's innate for most of us, even those who manufacture some type of alibi reasoning to explain what they did really wasn't wrong. That probably comes after they tried to hide the evidence of their works. Often not very well. They know to hide what they realize as bad and when they have done something wrong. There's not much difference with some racists who will seek to hide their actions and identity. Knowing what was done is bad. Once exposed they may have some type of alibi to explain what they did really wasn't wrong. Those participating in continuous racist patterns and practices will undoubtedly be classified at some point as being a racist. While those who unknowingly do similar acts as a result of their lack of knowledge, should probably not be classified as hate filled racist but should be provided knowledge so that their veil of ignorance is removed, allowing them to become respected members within our worldwide community. If after gaining knowledge they still practice racism, well then, they've made their choice.

For those having a limited knowledge of the various forms of racism that have been implemented throughout history or whose current views have changed over time, they face the possibility of becoming desensitized to some racist behaviors. What was once clearly classified as being racist, has somehow become a normalized behavior for them, providing what they honestly believe is their alibi. They will loudly proclaim, "I'm not a racist!" But in many cases, they just don't know it. However, they will be made aware since there will always be those for which racism has not become normalized, and they will call it as they see it. For those who have sunken to a level where racism has become normalized, you can expect they will be the first to deny any claims of being a racist. It's just how they have become accustom to behaving, while ignoring the feelings of those they have disrespected and caused pain. Their alibi of normalization has unknowingly presented a steep obstacle, and taken them far off the path of reaching an enlightened mind and developing agape. One example of normalization might be if you live in a town where one race has been deemed as only capable of handling low paid menial work. You might witness the people of that town treating many individuals of the targeted race as though none are deserving of higher paid jobs or capable of handling leadership or managerial jobs. This would be a racially biased generalization reinforced through biased hiring practices, while ignoring members within the same group who are continually awarded college degrees from the same institutions that other people in that town have attended. This scenario spotlights a normalization of racist behavior and the need for a conversation to better understand the motivation behind their continual actions and behaviors directed towards a specific race.

For anyone who has experienced being the target of racist behaviors, they usually have become skilled with recognizing derivatives initiated from the same or different sources. They also have begun to recognize it's not as easy to identify the motivating factors without having a conversation where those involved will engage in truthful discussions. In the absence of a truthful conversation it becomes a challenge to reach a healthy resolution or a change of negative behaviors.

For individuals who are sincerely interested in living their lives without intentionally inflicting harm to people, you may want to begin some self-analysis focused on identifying obvious gaps in your knowledge and understanding of racial groups you encounter on a regular basis, or which live in the same town or vicinity.

You can begin with your those who are in closest proximity and moving outward in concentric circles. Are there family members that are members of a different race whom you can ask if they would be comfortable sharing with you some personal experiences that could help you to gain perspective? Are there neighbors, acquaintances, co-workers, friends of friends that might be open to having proactive learning conversations? Would you feel comfortable organizing a small group over dinner where there can be a knowledge share focused on the group sharing, while learning more about practices one culture may not know about the other? Do you belong to organizations that resist diverse participation? When you look around your place of work does the workforce look similar to the community where it is located? If not, do you wonder why? Does the top to bottom management organizational structure include individuals from more than two races? What role do you play in supporting or maintaining this practice? Are you comfortable with the way things are, even after becoming aware of decisions being made that negatively impact one or more racial group?

Have you ever found yourself thinking "I don't like those people around me" or "I don't want them here"? A common practice is to contact some type of authority to communicate a concern or fear that in reality is motivated by hate or discomfort, with the hope the authority will forcibly remove the individual or group from your presence. Be gone! Many people may not realize throughout history at various points in time the same sentiment was expressed about individuals identified as Irish, Scottish, Chinese, Jewish, Christians, Muslims, Italian, Syrian, American Indian, Australian Aborigine, African, Mexican and many others around the world. In many cases, the attitudes of some were so consuming and contagious that collective actions were taken to forcibly relocate, isolate using embargoes, incarcerate, move entire groups to internment camps or engage in full out genocide. It's important to realize the motivating psychosis may be centered around the need for some to control who is around them and the need to live in an area where only one race of people thrives and exists. When you see a young person driving an expensive car depending on their race, do you think they belong to a privileged family, are trust fund babies or must be involved in criminal activities? When determining the political candidate of your choice would you prefer the one who proclaims they will be tough on crime? Historically when candidates purposely include tough on crime policy statements, those candidates are recognized as race baiting, using what is commonly referred to as a dog whistle to catch the attention of other racists. This strategy might be used to capture the votes of those who believe there are one or more distinct races or ethnic groups in their community who they believe and fear are consistently involved with criminal activities. As a result of these stereotypes and generalizations the expectation is the candidate will ensure specific groups will be policed more than other residents, and human rights violations may become normalized.

There's another racist tactic that has been quietly used by local media channels. This unwritten policy centers on protecting the reputation of specific individuals living in their community. Since crime is not exclusive and is found in all communities, media outlets often protect the reputation of those associated with some communities by not reporting their crimes or showing their picture when charged with a crime. For individuals belonging to those communities the media may tend to strictly follow the belief that people are innocent until proven guilty. And so, their reputations are protected. I've heard newscasters announce "a man has been charged" of a crime, making it difficult for viewers to know the race. However, this policy is not applied for individuals of all races. Also, in countless cases worldwide, the judicial systems have been known to ignore or be lenient to some groups, more than others. The impression that one race of people is consistently more involved with crime would be a racist generalization given the policy used by some media outlets and judicial systems to protect the reputation of specific groups. This policy also presents a danger to residents living in a community if crime has been increasing in their community but the media doesn't want a protected group to appear to be increasingly involved with criminal activity which if the public became aware could result in the lowering of property values as people begin to move out for their safety.

The glaring and obvious reality is our world is changing. The populations of various regions continue to become more diverse. As individuals from different races begin to learn we are more alike than racist would like for us to believe, those populations are gradually becoming more tolerant and less fearful of living with people of different races. In addition, over decades of time the former targets of racist patterns and practices have worked to gain economic and political power, advanced academically and are being elected and appointed into judicial positions. Simultaneously, the individuals and groups that resist learning how to live with others and continue to support efforts focused on establishing a world where there is only one race that gets all of the benefits, are becoming increasingly frustrated. Their anxiety is becoming openly apparent. So much that blatant racist acts, terrorist acts and hate crimes that were previously covertly devised within exclusive 'member only' back room meetings held in domestic legislative, judicial, media, economic, law enforcement and geo-political organizations are increasingly being exposed and mitigated. With the continuous shift in power, racists are losing more and more of their ability to control who will enjoy the abundant benefits that are available throughout this planet. For them, the world is getting out of control while for others, it's getting more enjoyable. The opportunities are expanding as more doors open and people are welcomed to share the rich and varied life of their neighbors.

In my opinion I believe if you knowingly conduct actions with intent to inflict harm on someone of a different race, you are a racist. If you are unknowingly involved with actions that inflicts harm on someone of a different race, you probably should not be labeled as a racist. Instead be made aware of the harm you delivered. If you continue after becoming aware, you should be labeled as a racist. Between each of those points of references can be many degrees.

I also believe societies will continually be challenged by pivotal events that will either make them stronger or will destroy bits and pieces until they are no longer recognized as the former. History has documented the fall of empires, continual evolution of needs and redistribution of power. The number of incidents centered around gun violence and hate crimes also go through cycles as the overall health of individual populations go through change. As the gun violence and hate crimes increase, those impacted are often the ones who will stand up and demand a change that provides safety. If leaders want to remain leaders they will respond to the needs of the people or should expect to eventually lose their power preferably by a non-violent transition of power.

When populations begin going down a path where there is an increasing loss of life to all members of its population, no matter their race, age, gender, economic status or privilege, that population is in the midst of an epidemic that could annihilate their most valuable resource, the people. Leaders can't wait too long to identify the cause, develop plans to mitigate the damage and place controls in place to ensure the problem doesn't return. After experiencing epidemic level events, most countries strengthen legislative controls, checks and balances to protect them from future cycles that could recur having more intensity and impact. It is a fight for survival that can't be taken lightly. It's also during these tests that leadership is assessed for their commitment to serving their constituents. The time it takes for them to fix problems will provide proof of their value while being in the positions of power. When populations see one race being impacted, leaders might display minimal urgency for mitigation of problems. But when the entire population begin to be impacted, constituents will collectively demand quick action. Gun violence and hate crimes directed at anyone who doesn't show allegiance to racism and hate is the type of disease that cannot be tolerated. Those who stand on the side of humanity, respect for the safety, health, opportunities and prosperity of all people and the long-term viability of their homeland, should be a primary objective. Those who work to destroy those high-level goals are threats to the health of the majority of people.

Closing Thoughts

I continue to learn by sharing my experiences and hearing about the experiences of others. To engage you need to have confidence in who you are and not be afraid of hearing something that you previously didn't know. That begins with asking questions, being comfortable with having an exchange of ideas, taking time to assess what you hear, and being slow to anger.

Racism often rides on the back of a horse called desire and conquest. The age of acquisition begins as a child. When you hear the words, "that's mine" followed by a shove, you should start adding to your list. Kids need to receive constant guidance on sharing with others, not needing to hoard everything they have, not coveting the toys that others have and learning socialization skills. Children need to be taught how to take some personal responsibility with facing and then working to identifying solutions to overcome their challenges. We all need problem solving skills and continual reinforcement to work at solving our problems, not sinking into a mental state where you feel someone else can block you from achieving your goals and expectations. It's absolutely true you will face individuals and institutionalized practices that could potentially hinder you. It's also absolutely true that no one can stop your ability to innovate and find ways around road blocks. There are an unlimited number of options that don't require extreme actions or reliance on one path or solution. Sun Tzu, the author of "The Art of War" recommends a number of antidotes for handling challenges. "In the midst of chaos, there is also opportunity." "The greatest victory is that which requires no battle." "Supreme excellence consists of breaking the enemy's resistance without fighting." These words from one of the most prolific military strategists in history, suggest challenges can be overcome without violence, but by using solutions that don't require physical conflict.

    Coveting, a word that is rarely spoken but seen daily. You want what they have. We are bombarded with commercials and are the target of endless marketing campaigns. It's a drug and we are addicted. Clothes, smart phone, money, social media followers, travel, cars, trucks, jewelry, tattoos, a house, furniture, physical enhancements, high income, acknowledgement, property, pets, freedom to do whatever and whenever we want. For some the desire to have what someone else has is so strong they will do almost anything to acquire and possess. Newton's third law of physics concludes for every action, there is an equal and opposite action. What could be considered to be the opposite force of acquisition? I personally think it should be charity. For each thing that you covet and acquire, you should practice charity. Establishing a cycle where you give away something of value each time you acquire something of value. This could provide some psychological balance and possibly diminish the anxiety caused when you feel you are losing out or not keeping up with the need to acquire something someone else has.

The sooner you recognize most people are facing challenges and obstacles that hinder them from fulfilling their desire to acquire and possess what others have, the sooner you can begin to plan a path that increases your own unique set of opportunities determined by your capabilities mixed with personality. Every day presents an opportunity to innovate and create something, physically or intrinsically, that will be of value to others. Today, take some time to build something, create anything that reinforces your ability to have control in your life without exhausting valuable time working on establishing controls over others. Be the entrepreneur over your life to have control without total reliance on others. You will quickly forget about the need to blame others for not acquiring what you want and showing charity to who you want.

Volunteer to help someone. This will give you first-hand exposure to the challenge others face. You can also use this time to learn about other cultures and find out about differences and commonalities.

The enlightening of the mind only requires your decision to do it. There's no one you can blame. You have total control for this decision.

Take some time to give thanks for what was given, what you have, and for what is to come. Start small with your breath. Give thanks for that. Give thanks for today, and all of the thoughts you can create. Give thanks for the future. For there's something you are thinking about today that will materialize in the future. The reinforcement will be the increased confidence gained each time you go forward after falling back. The fun will be discovering something new along the way that you never expected. Keep in mind, whether or not you believe what I just said, we all have a past, present and future. That's what we call life and you are allowed to create good things. You should also be mindful of how the bad things get destroyed and don't flourish. There's a reason why people try to conceal the bad things in their lives. Even kids know to hide bad things and show everyone the good things.

Appendix: Considerations

Discussion Tip: Discussions should center on having mutual respect for all participants. If conversations involve more than four participants, they should agree on some fair set of rules of engagement focused on ensuring each participant is allowed to thoroughly communicate their views without interruption and individuals are respected. You may want to appoint a timekeeper and set a time limit on how long each person can speak so one person can't dominate the conversation. Since it will be difficult to cover a lot in one discussion, try to plan a series of discussions and agree on topics for each.

Discussion Tip: Be honest.

Suggestion: Please don't start a conversation regarding racism by trying to convince participants that racism doesn't exist. I'm sure there will be one or more who will not take your participation as being serious. A brief internet search will return a large body of evidence that confirms racism has existed and continues to exist on every continent. As a result, many groups around the world have been the target of racism or have utilized racist practices.

Conversation Tip: People on every continent have been impacted directly or indirectly by racism. They seem to fall in one of these categories. 1) They just hate people for some reason. 2) They fear people possibly the result of a lack of information, lacking direct interaction, concern for potential repercussions, having guilt or shame knowing they or someone in their family or ancestors hurt others. 3) They feel uncomfortable around certain people, possibly due to generalizations, stereotypes, implicit bias or an impact to one or more customary practices. Hate and hurting others may not be motivators in this case. 4) They are naïve of knowing that they are doing something that has historically been associated as being a racist behavior. Hate, fear, wanting to hurt others and being uncomfortable around others are probably not motivators in this case.

Conversation Tip: During your conversation keep in mind individuals can be involved directly or indirectly with racist behaviors as a result of hate, fear, discomfort or normalcy. Since racism has been evident globally and continued to be practiced, take some time to consider the level of impact when considering any action you believe should be taken for you to navigate in the region where you live or work.

Conversation Tip: Try not to end a conversation as enemies but as individuals having different opinions on an extremely challenging topic.

Suggestion: Keep in mind racism is a characterization where you can be documented for either standing on the side of human decency or branded with reputational shame that could impact you and your family for generations. Once documented, history cannot be erased. It's your choice to decide how you want your family, associates and acquaintances to interact with you and remember you.

Suggestion: Use some private time to think about what you believe are the motivating factors that drives your personal beliefs and behaviors related to other races. Try to determine what you believe would be lost, what are the benefits and what are the detriments. Again, you should try to be honest because in many cases others often can see the impacts to groups in your community. They may not know the impacts to you as an individual. If you choose not to talk about the factors that motivate your views on racism, it's still good for you to recognize what is personally of value to you or what are the detriments. Those who are the targets and those who benefit directly or indirectly could be impacted negatively or motivationally.

Conversation Tip: After you have taken some time to think about what you believe has influenced you, consider sharing those influences during your conversations. I've found there are many people who have experienced something that hurt them or increased their fears enough to fortify their conviction to support one side or the other.

Suggestion: After sharing events that influenced your beliefs, ask others if they would share any of the motivating factors or events that influenced them to adopt their beliefs. Those factors may bring a bit of clarity to their actions.

Suggestion: Take some time to discover what is the history behind various racist practices, patterns and behaviors. The history of racism spans around the globe. So much so that many countries have implemented laws, some of which are vehemently enforced. Being unaware in this case could result in an unexpected ending to your travel plans.

Knowledge Tip: Psychiatrists and neuroscientists claim there is evidence that an individual's brain doesn't develop the capacity to be rational or understand the consequences of one's actions until some point around the age of 25. That means after the brain matures individuals may realize some of their previous actions have resulted in hurtful impacts to people. At that point they might decide to change their behavior. Could you be participating in activities that you will be ashamed of later? Possibly impact your reputation. Yes. Could you be passive with taking measures to ensure your rights are not violated? Might you have been passive by allowing someone to hurt or abuse you and later have to live with regret, shame or blaming yourself? Yes.

Knowledge Tip: Since research suggests toddlers, infants and young children can become gender and racially biased as a result of parents and the various environmental influences absorbed from the community where raised, parents should teach their children positive behaviors that are not harmful to others. Parents need to help them develop racial socialization skills and to have multi-cultural awareness. Encourage them to avoid racial, gender and class bias. Teach them to acknowledge their own race and traditions while having respect for other races that may have similar aspirations and love for their traditions. Help them to understand what is dignity, human decency, having respect for others, and civility. In the absence of parental guidance, they will learn from the environment where they live and adopt patterns and practices that they believe are normal. For example, a child who grows up in a home where they witness abuse may believe its normal. As an adult they might continue the abusive behaviors when interacting with others. A child growing up in a community where they witness high volumes of violence, may believe that's a norm for all communities. A child who grows up in a community where profanity is regularly used may believe using profanity is a normal way to communicate.

Questions for Your Consideration: Are you aware of some healthy options available that can assist with the psychological development of children and young adults who live in environments that have normalized hate and racist behaviors? What learning tools can be used to help them gain humanistic behavior skills, cultural awareness, socialization skills and be considerate to individuals of other races? If you don't know of any, you could start by asking local primary care providers for advice with where you can find information.

Questions for Your Consideration: Are you aware in the United States of America it has been estimated that roughly 2,000 children, from all races, are abducted daily. Bias is decided by the purchaser who could be a local or international criminal. What could you do to protect your children from being abducted and sold? Have you checked with local resources? Have you had a family talk, determined emergency locations, considered code words, martial arts training, panic alarms, GPS tracking devices that are physical or embedded?

Conversation Tip: Don't be afraid to acknowledge harmful practices that you may have been involved with directly or indirectly. Maybe you will be motivated to become active and get involved to correct them.

Conversation Tip: Try not to react with anger when someone has opposing views. Discussion presents the opportunity for you to gain better understanding about others, yourself or re-assess the validity of your current views. All of which should be a benefit to you.

Knowledge Tip: Having friends or acquaintances who are members of a different race does not mean that you would not participate directly or indirectly in racist patterns, practices or behaviors. Slave owners knew people belonging to a different race while concurrently utilizing the dehumanizing institution of slavery for social, economic and political gains. Currently there are countless numbers of businesses that support racist practices in hiring, redline pricing, avoidance of social responsibilities, lobbying in favor of 'Jim Crow' legislative initiatives and providing financial support to racist politicians. They engage in racism while simultaneously selling goods and services to those negatively impacted by racism. All focused on enhancing their wealth. These companies target individuals belonging to different races as consumers while at the same time disrespecting them as individuals. The institution of slavery dehumanized a workforce of free labor while relying on them to build wealth.

Conversation Tip: Don't expect everyone will acknowledge the pain they've caused others. That doesn't mean you shouldn't consider tolerance nor does that mean you should be tolerant of abusive dehumanizing behavior. Since racism extends globally, your approach to living in an environment filled with racism may include having some tolerance for those who believe in racist policies, but also determining what are your own healthy boundaries, goals, expectations and criteria needed for ensuring your prosperity.

Conversation Tip: Knowing that racism has the potential to evoke high levels of emotion in some people, you should avoid name calling, stereotyping, using language that is disrespectful, confrontational, inflammatory, embarrassing, inconsiderate and dehumanizing.

Conversation Tip: You may not be able to convince everyone of the harm created by racism. You can be successful pursuing a goal to enlighten others of your perspectives. However, you'll need fortitude. This goal can get old or become frustrating.

Conversation Tip: Try to close each conversation with a summary along with some type of a compromise and follow-up actions. Don't expect every conversation will result in change. Learn from the smallest gains. Try to arrange follow-up conversations that provides opportunities to gain additional understanding and potentially build new relationships.

Knowledge Tip: It's the nature for people to constantly strive towards eliminating painful and oppressive behaviors that restrict their ability to grow and have healthy, prosperous lives. It's also normal to have fears related to what you believe will negatively impact your future. To live with fear can result in anxiety and impact your health. If some of your fears are motivated by concerns for how your life might become negatively impacted if a specific race began to utilize power and wealth to hurt you, then you should consider multiple plans to avoid dependence on the specific race for your viability and success.

Knowledge Tip: The degree of dedication or conviction an individual has for acquiring and retaining power, wealth, privilege and access to resources can motivate the level of racism. Throughout history when one race of people is targeted with racist practices, most will develop strategies to circumvent or eliminate those practices.

Question for Your Consideration: As more individuals begin to start their own businesses and become entrepreneurs, they will no longer need to wait for a day in which there will be fair hiring and promotion practices in the workplace. Their proactive measures will result in their ability to remove their selves from the equation by diminishing the level of oppressive control by others. If your traditions and way of life is dependent on oppressing and treating others unfairly, what do you expect will happen to your livelihood as the oppressed develop ways to remove their selves from the equation and from oppression?

Questions for Your Consideration: When individuals, groups or businesses are publicly exposed as being racist, resulting in negative impacts to their reputation, income and customer base, do you believe those who are identified as being a racist will experience increased tension and anxiety? Do you think their increased anxiety will manifest into increasing numbers of hate crimes? Do you think business investors might conclude they need to change the way business leaders conduct business?

Knowledge Tip: Individuals can build upon their personal growth by learning conflict resolution techniques.

Question for Your Consideration: Upon recognizing that making a change in one's life and beginning behavior modification is difficult, what do you think are realistic options for individuals who decide to maintain their racist behaviors?

Question for Your Consideration: If you were working for an organization that provided service to a worldwide marketplace that includes various cultures but you only have a workforce comprised of individuals belonging to one race, do you believe your organization will be as competitive as organizations who have hiring practices focused on developing a diverse workforce?

Question for Your Consideration: Some countries have laws that prohibit biased hiring practices by employers, however those laws are rarely enforced. Since bias in hiring practices can be utilized against individuals of all races, what strategies could you initiate that ensures your ability to circumvent the practice of biased hiring?

Questions for Your Consideration: Implicit bias and racial profiling has resulted in individuals from all races being unfairly treated by police and judicial systems worldwide. For those who travel internationally or through communities controlled by authorities belonging to different races, they could experience unfair treatment or limited service. Do you think individuals who work in law enforcement and the judicial system should complete psychological assessment and screening for bias? Do you think implicit bias training should be completed before being allowed to work in law enforcement and judicial systems?

Questions for Your Consideration: If you are a business owner or business strategy leader, are you concerned with seeing your competitors increasing investments to diversify and expand their business footprint across various racial segments including international markets in-order to capture increasing amounts of profits and market share? How do you think your competition's strategy will impact your business' long-term viability and ability to maintain a vibrant workforce? Have you had internal discussions about enhancing key business communications, including your website, so that you can communicate in different languages? Do you employ client-facing resources who can converse in multiple languages?

Question for Your Consideration: Historically there have been a number of businesses who use their influence to lobby politicians to obtain legislative and tax advantages, while donating money and resources to organizations to encourage them to adopt specific policies. Some work to build a positive reputation in the communities they market while others orchestrate strategies to gain favors and benefits. Do you believe there is any benefit or value for businesses to use their influence to improve race relations in your region?

Questions for Your Consideration: As a result of the large amount of time employees spend daily under the supervision of workplace managers, some might consider the workplace environment as a place of continuing education that picks up from the early development period guided by parents and school teachers. Did you know most large businesses provide education courses and pay a portion of their employees' external education costs as part of their benefits package? Did you know a number of large corporations require as a formality, their employees to electronically confirm they will comply with corporate ethical policies? Since corporate ethical policies encourage their employees to avoid getting caught engaging in unethical behavior, including racism, do you think these corporations should expand their required training to include courses that facilitate humanistic behavioral values that could motivate how their employees interact with all people living in their communities?

Questions for Your Consideration: Do you think there is any correlation with increasing levels of anxiety being openly displayed by racists, people who encourage hate behaviors and the increase in mass shootings and hate crimes? What do you think are some solutions that could be implemented to lower the levels of anxiety and diminish the occurrence of mass shootings and hate crimes?

www.ingramcontent.com/pod-product-compliance
Lightning Source LLC
Chambersburg PA
CBHW020301030426
42336CB00010B/855